Incas

A Captivating Guide to the History of the Inca Empire and Civilization

© **Copyright 2017**

All rights Reserved. No part of this book may be reproduced in any form without permission in writing from the author. Reviewers may quote brief passages in reviews.

Disclaimer: No part of this publication may be reproduced or transmitted in any form or by any means, mechanical or electronic, including photocopying or recording, or by any information storage and retrieval system, or transmitted by email without permission in writing from the publisher.

While all attempts have been made to verify the information provided in this publication, neither the author nor the publisher assumes any responsibility for errors, omissions or contrary interpretations of the subject matter herein.

This book is for entertainment purposes only. The views expressed are those of the author alone, and should not be taken as expert instruction or commands. The reader is responsible for his or her own actions.

Adherence to all applicable laws and regulations, including international, federal, state and local laws governing professional licensing, business practices, advertising and all other aspects of doing business in the US, Canada, UK or any other jurisdiction is the sole responsibility of the purchaser or reader.

Neither the author nor the publisher assumes any responsibility or liability whatsoever on behalf of the purchaser or reader of these materials. Any perceived slight of any individual or organization is purely unintentional.

Free Bonus from Captivating History (Available for a Limited time)

Hi History Lovers!

Now you have a chance to join our exclusive history list so you can get your first history ebook for free as well as discounts and a potential to get more history books for free! Simply visit the link below to join.

Captivatinghistory.com/ebook

Also, make sure to follow us on:

Twitter: @Captivhistory

Facebook: Captivating History: @captivatinghistory

Contents

INTRODUCTION 1

CHAPTER 1 – HOW THE INCAS RECORDED THEIR HISTORY 3

CHAPTER 2 - THE INCA CREATION MYTH 7

CHAPTER 3 – THE FOUNDING OF THE GREAT CITY OF CUZCO 10

CHAPTER 4 - THE FIRST DYNASTY OF INCA RULERS AND THEIR GREATEST DEEDS 14

CHAPTER 5 - THE SECOND DYNASTY OF INCA RULERS AND THEIR GREATEST DEEDS 18

CHAPTER 6 – THE RISE OF THE INCA EMPIRE: A COSMOLOGICAL EVENT? 23

CHAPTER 7 – SOCIAL ORDER IN THE INCA SOCIETY 31

CHAPTER 8 – THE DIFFERENT ROLES OF WOMEN IN THE INCA SOCIETY 39

CHAPTER 9 – INCA RELIGIOUS ORDER AND IDEOLOGY 43

CHAPTER 10 – TOUR OF THE GREATEST INCA SIGHTS 50

CHAPTER 11 - FROM PACHACUTI TO THE ARRIVAL OF THE SPANISH 58

CHAPTER 12 – THE SPANISH CONQUEST 61

CHAPTER 13 - THE AFTERMATH AND THE INCA LEGACY 70

CONCLUSION 72

FREE BONUS FROM CAPTIVATING HISTORY (AVAILABLE FOR A LIMITED TIME) 75

ENDNOTES 76

ABOUT CAPTIVATING HISTORY 79

Introduction

One of the most notable ancient cultures of South America is undoubtedly the Inca Civilization. They once ruled over the largest empire in South America. Not only that - their empire was also the largest in the world at the time.

However, it didn't last long - within about a hundred years, the empire that stretched all the way from modern-day Quito, Ecuador in the north to modern Santiago, Chile in the south, lay in ruin. The Inca Empire that ruled over 10 million subjects was conquered by a few hundred Spanish conquistadors in the mid-16th century.

Despite its grand appearances, the Inca empire turned out to be weak and quickly disintegrated when the Spanish conquistadors arrived on their shores, with a measly force of 168 men, their leader Francisco Pizarro among them. How was this possible?

But there are many more mysteries surrounding the Incas. Where did the Incas originate? And how did they come to rule over their vast empire that incorporated mountaintops, tropical jungles, and coastal lands? What were the most notable achievements of their great kings? What did their temples and monuments look like, especially the capital city of Cusco and their breath-taking mountaintop settlement at Machu Picchu in modern-day Peru?

In this book, we'll discover what the Incas had for lunch, how their society was structured and their ideas about Cosmology and the origins of our world.

But before we embark on this journey of discovery, it's important to understand that the history of the Inca empire is not straightforward. The Incas did not have a linear concept of time. They were great orators though, and used stories to pass down oral history to their descendents. Therefore, most of their historical accounts come from Spanish sources or locals who learned Spanish and told the history of the Incas after the conquest.

Each chronicler had their motives and reasons for writing their story - some were seeking to get published, others wanted to justify the Spanish conquest, while others tried to portray the Inca empire as 'the golden age'. The Inca empire could be anything - a brutal totalitarian state that exploited its subjects, an organised system of rigid social structures, or a beautiful utopia.

We'll look at some accredited sources, specifically the work of one of the world's leading experts on Inca civilization Terence N. D'Altroy, Loubat Professor of American Archaeology in the Department of Anthropology and founding Director of the Center for Archaeology at Columbia University in the City of New York.

Chapter 1 – How the Incas Recorded Their History

For the Incas, the stories of their origins are so entangled with their myths and fables that it is difficult to discern fact from fiction. What's more, the Incas revered cosmology and the celestial bodies. Thus, many of their myths are better explained in relation to the movement of the planets, rather than the movement of people.

How the Incas recorded their history

Although they were one of the most sophisticated and advanced civilizations the Spanish Conquistadors encountered, they never developed writing.

Oral storytelling

The Incas had a particular class of individuals whose only duty was to memorise important events from the Inca history, recount them orally at courts or special events, and pass them onto the next generation. There were several issues with this. For example, the storyteller could omit or deliberately include specific events that happened to the previous Inca emperors, depending on whom he happened to be speaking to. What's more, these accounts usually detailed events from the lives of royalty, not the common folk.

Another problem for creating a chronological record of the history of the Incas, including the very beginnings of their civilization, was the Incas did not have a linear view of time. The chronicler and Jesuit missionary Padre Bernabé Cobo recorded the problems that arose when trying to construct a chronological history of the Incas in his book on the history of the Inca Empire.

> When they are asked about things of the past, if something happened more than four to six years ago, what they usually answer is that the incident occurred *ñaupapacha* which means 'a long time ago'; and they give the same answer for events of 20 years back, as for events of 100 or 1000 years back, except that when the thing is very ancient, they express this by a certain accent and ponderation of their words.

It is therefore difficult to ascertain any linear narrative from the oral history.

Quipus

Quipus were sets of knotted strings that helped the Incas communicate information and deal with numbers with remarkable precision and accuracy. What's more, this device was highly portable so that accurate records could be carried from place to place. The Incas used a variety of colours, strings and different types of knots tied at various ways and lengths to record and communicate important dates, accounts, and statistics. It was even used to record important episodes from folk tales, mythology, and poetry.

How did *quipus* record time and history?

The largest quipus ever found have as many as 1,500 strings of different colours, containing a number of knots that each held its specific meaning. As the method developed, a group of *quipu* masters or *quipucamayos* emerged. Their task was to memorise and keep an oral account that explained a particular *quipu*. This job was passed down from generation to generation. It wasn't an easy task; errors resulted in severe punishments.

Despite the sophistication, the materials used were simple - one needed to get some cotton or wool string and sometimes a wooden bar, from which the strings would hang. The strings had different colours. Each knot was thoughtfully placed in a designated spot. It was the combination of knots, colours and the length of each string that carried a particular meaning.

The method was based on a decimal positional system, counting as far as 10,000. Remarkably, this decimal system closely resembles that which we use in mathematics today. A knot could indicate a number if you counted the turns of the string within it. A knot tied in a figure-of-eight could indicate a fixed value, whereas a string that was missing a knot signified zero. There was also a way to suggest 'secondary strings' that meant this string was an exception or less important than the others.

You could tell what units were used on each *quipu* by looking at the strings placed furthest away from the primary string - this was the key to breaking the code of that particular *quipu*.

So, the Inca creation myth was perpetuated using oral storytelling and *quipus*.

The Spanish chroniclers

Later the history of the Inca and their myths were recorded by the Spanish chroniclers, each of whom had their own agenda, representing the stories in a different light. Many believed the Inca myths and beliefs to be a form of heresy for the Christian faith, and the judgement that the Spaniards imparted when presenting the native accounts resulted in historical inaccuracies.

Some years after the conquest, the Spanish chroniclers started to interview the local Andean people to get a better picture of their past. However, by this time much of their history was skewed towards a biased 'golden era' representation of the Inca rule. This is because the conditions that the locals endure under the Spanish rule were so catastrophic, compared to the treatment they'd received from the Inca rulers.

The first fifty to one hundred years of the Spanish rule are remembered as a 'black time' for the native people of the Andes. The Spanish continued to rage war against the last surviving Inca rulers, as well as fighting each other in a quest for more wealth and power. This left the locals in a difficult position, always torn between the military attacks of the surviving Incas and the Spanish conquistadors with no support from a united, consistent government. Even after the last indigenous Inca ruler Túpac Amaru was decapitated in 1572, the internal conflicts among the Spanish continued, shunned by the King of Spain. Within forty years of the initial Spanish appearance, the local population of the Inca empire had fallen by 50%, with the coastal population suffering the most. A combination of civil wars, forced labour and pestilence that raged for almost one hundred years, made the locals crave for a 'golden age' of the Inca rule and idealise it.

Here are some of the most notable Spanish chroniclers where much of our knowledge of the Incas today comes from:

- Juan de Betanzos's *Narrative of the Incas* (written in the 1550s).
- Bernabé Cobo's *History of the Inca Empire* (1653).

- Garcilaso de la Vega's *El Inca, Royal Commentaries of the Incas, and General History of Peru* (1609).
- Felipe Guaman Poma de Ayala's *El primer nueva corónica y buen gobierno* (written around 1615).

Chapter 2 - The Inca Creation Myth

Similar to other cultures that existed in South America, there was a creator god who created several tribes. The Incas called him Viracocha Pachayachachi, which means 'The Creator of all things.' The Incas believed Viracocha emerged from the waters at Lake Titicaca, creating the earth and the sky before he returned to the waters.

While the age of darkness still ruled over the Earth, he fashioned his first creation - giants made from stone and rocks and gave them special orders that had to be revered.

The Great Flood

But things didn't go as smoothly as Viracocha had planned. The people he'd created kept his orders for a while. After some time though, vice and pride crept among the hearts of the men he'd created, and they stopped following the creator god's orders, preferring to do as they pleased.

As a result, Viracocha cursed them - he turned some of them into stone and other things, and ordered the earth and the sea to swallow the others. Similar to many other creation stories, a great flood swallowed up the earth, known as *uñu pachacuti* or 'water that overturns the land.'

According to some versions, it rained for 60 days and 60 nights, drowning all creation. Some of the giants that were turned back to stone could be seen at sites like Tiahuanaco (or Tiwanaku) and Pukará. Some of the nations are said to have survived, saved from the flood to create the next generation of men.

The second attempt of creation

Viracocha then made a second attempt at creation of man. Still, in the age of darkness, he created people, fashioning them out of clay. He gave them language, agriculture, the arts, and clothes, after which he created all kinds of animals. He told these first people (known as *Vari Viracocharuna*) to populate all corners of the world, but he left them to live inside the Earth.

Viracocha also decided to create the celestial bodies, such as the Sun, the Moon and the stars to bring the world out of the age of darkness and bestow light upon men and all living beings. He used the islands in Lake Titicaca to fashion these heavenly bodies.

Viracocha decided to create another group of men, called *viracochas*. He made these people memorise all the different characteristics of the races and cultures of people that would later populate the world. He sent all the *viracochas* out of the womb of the Earth, leaving two behind. The ones who left, went to all kinds of habitats - caves, streams, rivers, waterfalls - each making the place their home, as Viracocha had ordered them. When they arrived in each settlement, they instructed the people who already lived there that it was time to emerge from the depths of the Earth.

Viracocha ordered all the men to populate every corner of the world, and to live without quarrels, in perfect harmony with each other. He also ordered them to serve him and observe a specific covenant they were not to break, lest they are confounded.

Satisfied, Viracocha spoke to the two people who'd remained and asked them to go forth and help him spread the new civilization far and wide. One of them ventured eastward to Andesuyo, and the other went west, to a region known as Condesuyo. They were instructed to awaken the people they'd meet on their way.

The journey of Viracocha

As for Viracocha, he went towards the great city of Cuzco, dressed in beggar's clothes. He took on different names, such as Con Ticci Viracocha, Atun-Viracocha, and Contiti Viracocha Pachayachachic. He travelled the world, imparting valuable knowledge about the arts, civilization, language and other studies. According to some accounts, he was assisted by his two sons or brothers - depending what version of the myth you hear - Imaymana Viracocha and Tocapo Viracocha. However, they were not always welcome - some people went as far as to stone Viracocha.

For example, on his way to Cuzco, he encountered people who lived in the province of Cacha. He awakened the Canas people there who emerged from the depths of the Earth but did not recognize the Creator God. They attacked him. But after Viracocha made fire rain from a nearby mountain, they flung themselves at his feet, and

Viracocha forgave them.

He then founded the great city of Cuzco, awakening people known as the Orejones - they are said to have been wearing huge golden discs in their earlobes - and they consequently became the rulers of Cuzco.

Eventually, Viracocha made it all the way to Manta, Ecuador and then crossed the Pacific waters, meeting the other *viracochas* along the way. He headed into the West, promising to return one day. Before he left, he told men to beware of 'false men' who would claim that they were *viracochas*.

What can the creation myth tell us about the Incas?

Although little historical evidence exists to confirm the credibility of any part of the Inca creation myth, it is nonetheless important to note as it gives an insight into the mind of an Inca and how their society functioned. For example, the various places from which the Inca emerged - such as waterfalls, springs, and caves - were regarded as sacred, and worshipped by the Incas. They called these sites *huacas,* and believed that a semi-divine spirit inhabited them, often erecting shrines there.

They built special shrines in the places believed to have been visited by Viracocha. For example, where he sent fire to rain over the Canas people, the Inca built a shrine. They also built a bench made of solid gold to hold a statue that Viracocha was believed to have erected at Urcos when he journeyed there. This is also significant because Francisco Pizarro who led the Spanish inquisition later claimed the bench as part of his share of the conquest.

The creation myth also sheds important insight into how the Incas treated other cultures. Although the Incas later built a massive empire that had roughly 10 million subjects, ruled by only 100,000 Incas, they did not impose their religion and statutes over the cultures they conquered. Instead, they incorporated the specific beliefs of each culture into the fabric of their own culture. This was mostly to do with Viracocha's message that tribes had their distinct characteristics that he had created for a purpose, and should therefore all live in harmony. This is very different to the Spanish conquistadors who later tried to impose Christianity upon their conquered subjects.

Chapter 3 – The Founding of the Great City of Cuzco

The city of Cuzco, located in ancient Peru, was one of the most important cities for the Incas. The Incas called it 'The navel of the Universe' and the city flourished between c. 1400 and 1534 AD. During its peak years, Cuzco had as many as 150,000 inhabitants. It was a spectacular city, rich with wondrous buildings and temples, dedicated to their gods.

But how did the Incas arrive at Cuzco?

The Incas epic journey to Cuzco

At the time of the Spanish invasion, the Incas believed that they had only had 13 generations of rulers. They believed their original ancestors were created by the god Viracocha from the sun god Inti. This is where the name 'Inca' comes from - they considered themselves to be 'children of the Sun.' Their ruler, in turn, was the Sun god Inti's embodiment on Earth.

The very first Inca ruler and human, according to their mythology, was Manco Capac. Although he founded the city of Cuzco, he was not originally from there. Following the orders from Viracocha, he journeyed to Cuzco with his *sister and wife* Mama Ocllo, accompanied by three other couples who were also siblings.

One version of the myth tells that the four original couples emerged from a sacred cave. Instructed by Viracocha, they journeyed north for about 30km. Not all of them made it there, though.

One of the siblings turned out to have a spiteful and mean character, and so the others tricked him to return to the cave and then rolled a large boulder in front of him, so he remained forever trapped. Another brother was turned into a stone pillar along the way, and yet another was transformed into a pillar at Cuzco.

When the Incas arrived at Cuzco, they discovered it was inhabited by a tribe called Chanca. Nonetheless, Viracocha gave them a sign in a giant rainbow across the sky, to indicate this truly was their promised land. Aided by his promise, and with the help of some stone warriors, the original Incas defeated them. Upon victory, Manco Capac threw a golden rod at the ground and founded the city of Cuzco, consequently becoming the first Inca ruler.

These are the mythical origins of the Inca civilization - but is there any truth in this story?

What archaeology can tell us

Archaeological evidence found in the valley of Cuzco shows that the first settlements were established as early as 4500 BC. The valley was inhabited by hunter-gatherers, who lived in small communities.

However, it wasn't until 500 BC the population settled and made Chanapata their primary dwelling place. Although archaeological digs in the area have produced some evidence of decorated pottery, no evidence has been found from this period to suggest the existence of large buildings, art or metalwork.

At about 1000 AD, these small communities occupied an area of about 60km. The largest towns at the time housed a few thousand people. The central point for these communities was Cuzco. This period is known as Killke or the pre-imperial Inca era. Archaeological evidence shows at around 1200 AD this area was relatively peaceful, however there were some minor conflicts among the communities.

As the years went on, Cuzco became more important to the Incas. From 1200 CE onward the great city began to take shape. Led by their leaders, the Incas began a determined unification of the communities late in the 14th century. According to historical accounts, the Incas did rage war against the Chanca people and defeated them in 1438 AD. This was when Cuzco became the capital of the Inca empire that continued to expand in all directions.

Eventually, it stretched across the Andes, as the Inca conquered many other cultures in their quest for greatness, becoming the largest empire in the Americas and the largest empire in the entire world at that time. Cuzco was the religious and administrative centre of this vast empire, where all the power and wealth derived from taxes was consolidated.

The wealth was evident in Cuzco - each Inca ruler left a grand legacy behind them, complete with their unique palace and a walled residential complex – as well as spectacular temples dedicated to their gods. The city was greatly expanded in the mid-15th century, during the Inca ruler Pachacuti Inca Yupanqui's reign.

Why was Cuzco so important?

With such a vast empire, any city could have become the administrative centre for the Incas. The Incas chose Cuzco. Mythology aside, why was this city so advantageous to them as to be selected as their capital?

Geographically, the city is located on an ancient glacier lake bed (hence the name 'dried-up lake bed'). It is situated in a conveniently and politically advantageous central point between many natural routes, each leading to a different region within the empire.

Several rivers meet in Cuzco, too. Namely, the Huatanay, Tellme, and Chinchilla. For the Incas, this was not only advantageous but held a particular significance also - it was a sign of good fortune. They did tamper with nature a little - the Incas canalized and diverted the rivers to create the space they needed for building their great city. However, they held a firm belief that nature could be adapted but must never be abused.

The valley itself is located at a high altitude, about 3,450m high, surrounded by picturesque mountain peaks. Despite the high altitude, the valley was still a fertile place to grow crops. The hills provided excellent pasture for the domesticated animals.

Thanks to its naturally advantageous location and the Incas creation myth, Cuzco was regarded as a sacred site. Later as the Inca empire expanded, their subjects were made to send tributes to Cuzco in the form of gold, precious artworks and valuable artefacts, and even people. Some came willingly, others as hostages. For example, expert craftsmen and skilled artists were ordered to relocate to Cuzco. Other hostages became sacrificial victims.

To boost the notion of their great city being 'the navel of the Universe,' the Incas improved the natural roads and passages by building paved roads and 41 sacred sight lines. They also had their version of propaganda - miniature models of Cuzco were circulated around their vast empire to show off the wealth and size of their capital.

And yet, the city was sacked by the Spanish conquistadors in the mid-16th century, with the last Inca ruler being executed in 1533. What could have led to such a rapid downfall?

Chapter 4 - The First Dynasty of Inca Rulers and Their Greatest Deeds

The Inca had a special name for their rulers. They called them 'Sapa Inca' or 'Inca Qhapaq.' Translated, these terms mean 'the only Inca' or 'mighty Inca.' They also used the name 'Apu' which means 'divinity.' The Inca saw their rulers as direct descendants of the god of Sun, known as Inti.

Manco Cápac (c. 1200 to 1230 AD)

This lineage began with their very first ruler Manco Cápac. He was the one who, according to myths, journeyed all the way to Cuzco valley and founded the great Inca city. The Inca rulers who succeeded him wore *mascapaycha,* a ceremonial band of red wool on their foreheads, with fringed tassels of gold thread. This headware had a symbolic meaning - whoever was wearing it held the most power in all the Inca kingdom.

The Inca rulers can be divided into two dynasties.

The Húrin dynasty

There is little historical evidence regarding the rulers from the first of these two dynasties - except their rule did not extend much further than the Kingdom of Cuzco. Manco Cápac was succeeded by his son.

Sinchi Roca (c. 1230 – 1260 AD)

According to one version of the Inca foundation myths, it was Sinchi Roca, the son of Manco Cápac, who led his entire family to the valley of Cuzco. His father named him as the successor to his throne, instructing him to care for his children and their descendants.

He is believed to have married Mama Cura, who came from the lineage of Sanu and together they had a son Sapaca. She may have been his sister which would have been a tradition at the time.

Sinchi Roca was a peaceful man and did not get involved in military exploits. Except when a situation called for prompt action, as in the case of Teuotihi. He was a diplomat the Incas had sent to a neighbouring kingdom to deliver a critical message. Ignoring the peaceful gesture, their neighbours killed Teuotihi and sent his head to Cuzco in reply. Thus, a war ensued, culminating in the Battle of Mauedipi where the Incas won a decisive victory.

Legends say the Inca kingdom expanded at this point, but no supportive archaeological evidence has been found thus far in favour of this claim. It is believed that no lands were added to the Inca kingdom during the reign of Sinchi Roca.

Instead, most of his efforts were focused on improving the land and the lives of people in Cuzco. According to the accounts of the chronicler Pedro Cieza de Leóne, Sinchi Roca improved the fertility of the land in the valley by building terraces and importing large quantities of soil. While his father and mother were still alive, Sinchi Roca also erected the House of the Sun.

An unusual part of his legacy is that his name *sinchi* came to signify a local ruler while his father's name *cápac* became a title that was given to warlords.

When it was time to hand over the throne to his successor, Sinchi Roca did something unusual. As opposed to his father, he named his youngest, rather than eldest son Lloque Yupanqui as the next ruler.

Lloque Yupanqui (c. 1260 – 1290 AD)

Just like his father Lloque Yupanqui was not interested in wars, so no additional lands were added to the Inca kingdom. He focused on making the kingdom better from within. During his reign, he succeeded in establishing a public market in Cuzco.

He also built an educational institution, Acllahuasi. Translated, it means 'the house of the chosen ones.' It was a centre for educating women. Later, when the Inca kingdom had grown to the size of an Empire, Acllahuasi gathered young women from all corners of the land.

Mayta Cápac (c. 1290 – 1320)

Until Mayta Cápac's reign, there was no real need to initially expand the Kingdom of Cuzco.

There were numerous reasons for expanding the Inca empire, but one possible explanation is drought. Some of the farmlands in the Cuzco valley were either abandoned or simply less productive than previously. To maintain their standard of living, the Incas had no choice but to go out and conquer new lands that would provide them with the necessary resources.

Mayta Cápac was the right man for the job. As opposed to his more peaceful predecessors, he was described as an aggressive youth, inclined towards fighting from a young age. According to the chroniclers Pedro de Cieza de León and Pedro Sarmiento de Gamboa, some of the war conflicts for the Incas during Mayta Cápac's reign started as a quarrel between him and some boys from a neighbouring group. It is not clear who started it first, but one of the parties was guilty of stealing some water from the other. The disagreement escalated into a war that Mayta Cápac, now a ruler, won. Following their success, the Inca soldiers looted homes, captured lands and imposed a tribute on their enemies.

Mayta Cápac was very young when he assumed the throne. Therefore his father's brother was named as the regent until he came of age.

With his wife Mama Cuca, Mayta Cápac had many children, including his successor Tarco Huamán. He was to become his rightful heir, but Tarco Huamán's reign was short. After a few short years, his cousin Cápac Yupanqui instigated a coup in his palace and took the throne by force.

Cápac Yupanqui (c. 1320 – 1350 AD)

Cápac Yupanqui was the last ruler of the Húrin dynasty. He was known as the 'splendid accountant Inca.' His elder brother Cunti Mayta earned himself an important title, too - he became the high priest of the Inca kingdom.

Cápac Yupanqui is remembered as a man who imposed a Draconian administration upon the Inca kingdom. His first act was to proclaim a death sentence upon the nine surviving siblings of Tarco Huamán, to ensure that no one could contest with his claim for power. He also expelled some of the Inca from the city. His claim to power was supported by his lineage to Mayta Cápac, who was his uncle.

According to the chronicler Juan de Betanzos, Cápac Yupanqui was the first Inca ruler to conquer territories outside of the Cuzco valley. The legends surrounding him commemorate him as a fierce warrior. He occupied the region of the *Cunti* in the north and *Colla* in the south.

Following this, another tribe known as *Quechua* asked for his assistance in their war against *Chanca of Andahuayllas*. After successfully defeating them, Cápac Yupanqui expanded his influence further upon the region.

But he was more than just a warlord. According to the chronicler Garcilaso de la Vega, Cápac Yupanqui also made many significant improvements within Cuzco. These included numerous buildings and bridges, new roads and even aqueducts that conveyed water to the inhabitants of the city.

However, things did not end well for Cápac Yupanqui. After conquering the lands of *Cuyo* and *Anca* some 22 km from Cuzco, Cápac Yupanqui felt inconvincible. He managed to make allies of another dominant force, the *Ayarmaca*. Threatened by the growing power of the Inca kingdom, their ruler offered his daughter as a wife.

The Inca rulers could have thousands of wives, and Cápac Yupanqui was no exception. His decision to marry again enraged one of his principal wives Cusi Chimbo. Allying herself with Inca Roca who belonged to an opposing faction and later became a successor to the throne, Cusi Chimbo poisoned her husband.

Chapter 5 - The Second Dynasty of Inca Rulers and Their Greatest Deeds

Cápac Yupanqui was the last Inca ruler from the Hurin dynasty. His rightful heir Quispe Yupanqui was killed in a rebellion between the *hanan* and *hurin* lineages, who elected Inca Roca as their ruler. He became the first ruler of the Hanan dynasty.

Inca Roca (c. 1350 – 1380 AD)

Inca Roca was proclaimed king after the Temple of the Sun was invaded by his supporters. Accounts about Inca Roca's parentage vary but he is believed to have been the son of Cápac Yupanqui with another wife.

Inca Roca was quick to marry his father's wife Cusi Chimbo and just as quickly poisoned her. He left the Temple of the Sun to the High Priest and built himself a palace complex to display his power. The remains of his palace still exist today - the walls of his palace can be seen in the Plaza de Armas in Cuzco.

Using clever diplomacy tactics, Inca Roca succeeded in ending many of the inter-ethnic disputes within the Inca kingdom and started to take on the neighbouring groups. He conquered the *Masca, Pinagua, Quiquijana* and even *Caitomarca* that was located some 30km from Cuzco. However, he ended up losing *Caitomarca* because he did not put any garrisons there. Inca Roca's tribe was a small ethnic group who saw their military exploits as an opportunity to plunder and pillage, rather than the annexation of the territories they conquered.

And then, a misfortune befell Inca Roca. His son Tito Cusi Huallpa whom he'd named as his successor, was taken hostage by the *Ayarmaca* who fought against the Inca and the *Huallacan* (who'd given one of their princesses as a wife to Inca Roca, even though she was promised to one of the *Ayarmaca* rulers). However, the conflict was resolved and peace celebrated among all the ethnic groups before Inca Roca died, and Tito Cusi Huallpa was safely returned to his rightful place as his father's heir.

Yáhuar Huácac (c. 1380 – 1410 AD)

Yáhuar Huácac was the name Tito Cusi Huallpa adapted after he took the throne. It means 'the one who cries bloodied tears' and its symbolism originates in the tale of his capture by the *Ayarmaca*.

Ayarmaca kidnapped Yáhuar Huácac when he was eight. This is because his mother Mama Mikay had initially been promised to one of their leaders before she married Inca Roca. She was a *Huayllaca* woman, and as revenge, the *Ayarmaca* decided to go to war with *Huayllaca*. To end this, *Huayllaca* gave her son Yáhuar Huácac to the *Ayarmaca,* and the group held him captive for many years.

Yáhuar Huácac cried tears that looked like real blood over his sad fate. His abductors were astounded by the miracle and soon became very fond of Yáhuar Huácac because of his charming personality.

He assumed the throne after his escape from captivity at 19, aided by one of his captor's mistresses Chimpu Orma. According to some sources, Yáhuar Huácac conquered Pillauya, Choyca, Yuco, Chillincay, Taocamarca, and Cavinas, adding them to the Inca kingdom.

However, Yáhuar Huácac's troubles didn't end there. Both he and the son he'd named as his successor was murdered. The elders were left to choose the next ruler.

Viracocha Inca (c. 1410 – 1438 AD)

Viracocha Inca assumed the name of the creator god after allegedly seeing visions of the creator god in Urcos. He went further still. After he took the throne, he was quick to declare he'll "conquer half of the world." He was described as warlike yet valiant, and his two captains Apu Mayta and Vicaquirau succeeded in subduing the lands within eight leagues of Cuzco. What's more, he was considered to be the first Inca ruler who ruled over the territories he conquered, as opposed to his predecessors who had merely raided or looted the territories without much further action.

Despite this, Viracocha Inca was threatened by the Chankas who had a similar force to the Incas. He fled Cuzco after his advisors told him to do so during a particularly fierce Chanka attack. According to the chronicler Juan de Betanzos, the Chankas justified the invasion by stating that they were offended by the Inca ruler taking on the name of the Creator god. He took some of his sons with him, but one of them rebelled against his father's decision. Cusi Inca Yupanqui said that he would not abandon Cuzco and the House of the Sun during this crisis. The night before the battle, he apparently had a vision from the gods, showing that during tomorrow's battle even the stones would raise up to lead the Incas into victory. Together with his brother Inca Rocca and six other chiefs, Cusi Inca Yupanqui defeated the Chankas.

But instead of being pleased with his son, Viracocha Inca was furious and refused to accept the spoils. (In the Inca tradition, this was usually done by the king walking on the heads of the defeated enemies.) He was so furious, in fact, he named another son as his successor and ordered for someone to kill Cusi Inca Yupanqui.

But his son survived and changed his name to Pachacuti or 'the turner of the earth.' He spent 20 years rebuilding Cuzco to be in the shape of a Puma. Pachacuti did pay a visit to his father and even invited him to come to Cuzco. When he did, Pachacuti greeted him with insults. He told him he had acted as a cowardly woman and had no right to rule. Viracocha abdicated his throne in favour of Pachacuti, and spent the rest of his days in an estate built especially for him.

Pachacuti (c. 1438 - 1471 AD)

Now we finally come to the Inca Empire or *Tawantinsuyu* (meaning 'four parts together') that was established by Pachacuti.

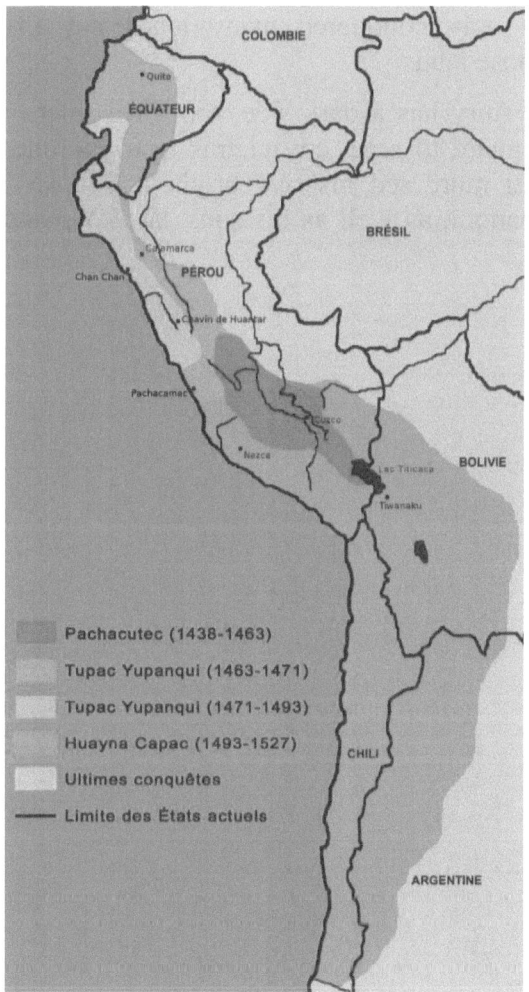

Map of the Inca Empire

https://commons.wikimedia.org/wiki/File:Inca-expansion_fr.png

Aside from being known as the 'turner of the earth,' Pachacuti was also known as 'the earth shaker' or 'he who overturns space and time.' Although the Inca rulers before him had their fair share of conquests, Pachacuti was the one who began an era of conquest. Within the next three generations, the Inca Empire would spread from the valley of Cuzco to almost all western South America. This included many ethnic groups and states. Thanks to his success, numerous epic stories have been created and told for centuries about Pachacuti's success. He's recognized by many as the true 'son of the Sun.' He not only conquered many lands but also added Inca garrisons in those lands.

However, his story has a dark side, too. Inca rulers always had to stay on their guard to repel any claims to the throne. This may be why Pachacuti murdered his two brothers Ccapac Yupanqui and Huayana Yupanqui, as well as his sons Tilca Yupanqui and Auqui Yupanqui.

Chapter 6 – The Rise of the Inca Empire: A Cosmological Event?

It took only 90 years for the Incan Empire to grow from 100,000 inhabitants to a force of 10 million. What was the key to its success? And why did this vast army practically surrender to the comparatively tiny Spanish force?

Dr. William Sullivan, a scholar of Native American cultures, has dedicated his entire life to unlocking the secret to the abrupt fall of the Incan Empire. In an extraordinary study presented in his book *The Secret of the Incas: Myth, Astronomy, and the War Against Time* and Timeline's Ancient Civilization Documentary *The Secrets of the Incas,* Dr Sullivan argues that the rise and the fall of the Incan Empire could be explained by the events that took place in their skies.

While they did not have a sophisticated system for writing, the Incas encrypted the biggest events from their history in the oral myths that were passed on from generation to generation, and are still being told in Peru today. Dr. Sullivan's study of these myths as a way to decipher the prophecies that the Incas perceived in the night sky, brings this culture closer to home, giving it a more human touch than mere historical accounts.

The importance of Cosmology in farming practices

To a modern mind, it is perhaps difficult to grasp the full significance that the alignment of planets and stars had on the mind of the Incas. We rarely venture outside to look at the stars, and when we do, often we can't see fully see them because of the pollution. Gazing at the night sky is indeed one way to put things into perspective, to transcend the day-to-day nuisances that trouble us, and to feel as though we are part of something much bigger than ourselves.

In stark contrast to us, the Incas lived and breathed nature and astronomy. They had incredibly sophisticated ideas of the night sky, considering the tools they had at their disposal. Although they did not linearly measure time as we do today, the Inca farmers relied on their observations in nature when it came to planning when to plant and harvest their crop.

For example, they observed the movement of the constellations to predict climate changes. Namely, the onset of a phenomenon we call El Niño - a band of warm ocean water that develops in the central and east-central equatorial Pacific at irregular intervals (every two to seven years). It causes global climate shifts, such as intense storms in some places and droughts in others.

The Incas knew they couldn't prevent it from happening, but they could prepare for it. To prepare themselves for El Niño and protect their crop, the Inca developed a way of predicting the onset of the phenomena so they could start their agricultural year earlier, raising their irrigation systems.

They used a method that is still in use by traditional potato farmers in Peru today. In June, six months before Christmas when the pool of warm water caused by El Niño is at its warmest in the Pacific waters near South America, they watch the night sky. If the star cluster known as Pleiades or Seven Sisters is clear, the farmers plant their crop as usual.

However, if it is obscured by atmospheric clouds, the farmers know that drought is likely to occur. To ensure that their crop survive, they adjust the planting dates of potatoes, their most important crop.

The Milky Way and its constellations

Dr. Sullivan's research suggests the Incas did not only rely on the stars to inform them of changing weather patterns - Cosmology was at the very heart of the Inca civilization.

The Incas saw everything that happened on Earth as an expression of what was happening in the sky above them. They had a corresponding practical action to everything that took place in the sky - on Earth; they worked hard to grind their crops with a millstone. Similarly, the gods ground the fate of the Incas in the sky.

Some of their creation stories also state that after their creator god Viracocha shaped the original few men and women out of clay, he asked them to emerge from 12 different places. So, they became 12 tribes, each representing a different constellation. Inca was one of these tribes. They were all to exist in perfect harmony and work with each other just like the 12 constellations worked in harmony in the night sky.

The constellations in their understanding of the Universe had different names to what we know of them today. These are the names the Inca gave to the central "dark cloud" constellations of the Milky Way (which they believed was the causeway linking men to gods) and their corresponding myth.

Mach'acuay - the Serpent

Mythology: For the Inca, snakes were mythological creatures. They even believed rainbows to be a type of snake.

Location: The *Mach'acuay* constellation is located on the Milky Way between the Southern Cross and Canis Major.

Time of appearance: For the Incas, the Serpent constellation emerges in August with its head-first and starts to set in February.

Interesting fact: Believe it or not, the few snakes that do inhabit the Andean areas become more active during the rainy season which takes place between December and February.

Hanp'atu - the Toad

Mythology: The Toad was an equally important mythological animal to the Incas, just like the Serpent.

Location: *Hanp'atu* can be seen in the night sky, chasing the Serpent away in August; it's a sort of dark cloud set between the Southern Cross and the Serpent's tail.

Time of appearance: This segment of the Milky Way becomes visible in Peru in August, signifying the start of the planting season.

Interesting fact: The toads who inhabit the Andean areas become more active when the rainy season is on, croaking more loudly when their constellation rises in the sky.

Yutu - the Tinamous birds

Mythology: Tinamous are birds that resemble partridges, commonly found in the Andean region. These birds eat small lizards and frogs, echoing the myth that the constellation *Yutu* chases *Hanp'atu* (the Toad) away.

Location: Yutu is the next constellation to emerge - it's a kite-shaped spot.

Time of appearance: *Yutu* emerges in its full glory when the Milky Way becomes visible in the night sky.

Interesting fact: After mating, the Tinamous female bird flees the nest and leaves the male to incubate the eggs - they may come from as many as five different males!

Urcuchillay - the Llama

Mythology: Arguably, *Urcuchillay* was the most important constellation for the Inca. Similarly, llamas were significant to the Inca - they provided food, served as a mode of transport for carrying goods and as sacrifices to the Inca deities.

Location: The constellation rises after the *Yutu,* and consists of llama mother and llama baby.

Time of appearance: *Urcuchillay* rises in November, with the two stars Alpha Beta Centauri serving as its "eyes."

Interesting fact: Llama sacrifices usually took place during critical astronomical events, such as the equinox or solstice.

Atoq - the Fox

Mythology: Andean foxes eat baby vicuñas, close relatives of llamas. But when this happens, the adult vicuñas team up and try to trample the foxes to stop them stealing their babies.

Location: The *Atoq* appears at the foot of the llama as a small black splodge.

Time of appearance: The Sun passes through this constellation in December.

Interesting fact: Andean baby foxes are born in December.

You may have noticed the interesting coincidence between the events on Earth (such as foxes being born when the constellation of Fox rises in the night sky). To the Inca, this was no coincidence, but rather yet another reminder of the interconnectedness of all matter.

According to Gary Urton, Dumbarton Oaks Professor of Pre-Columbian Studies at Harvard University: "The universe of the Quechuas is not composed of a series of discrete phenomena and events, but rather there is a powerful synthetic principle underlying the perception and ordering of objects and events in the physical environment."

What's more interesting is that many of the Inca temples in modern-day Peru resemble these constellations in how they were built. For example, there was a huge building built in the shape of *Yutu,* just beneath where that constellation would rise in the sky. It is still a great mystery as to how the Incas could be so precise and construct these temples so accurately. What is certain, however, is the extent of the Inca devotion to astrology.

Cosmology as a means to predict events on Earth

Now, picture what would have happened if people like the Inca, steeped so deep in cosmology and so reverent of their gods, suddenly discovered there had been a shift in the night sky. For instance, if Yutu could no longer be seen on the Milky Way, or if Urcuchillay did not rise in its usual place. For the Inca, this could mean only one thing - that the causeway between men and gods had been severed, and a major change was coming their way - an unwelcome change.

Dr. Williams had used several techniques for comparing various myths that he's come across during his travels to the Peruvian mountains with the way the constellations would have looked hundreds of years ago when the ancient Inca looked up at the night sky. He believes astrological phenomena coincided with the onset of an 800-year-long civil war in the Andean area back in 650 AD.

He also believes the Inca observed an even more significant astrological phenomena in 1442 AD, roughly 100 years before the arrival of the Spanish conquistadors. Whereas the previous sighting prophesied the onset of a long war, this next sighting foretold the end of the Incas, a break with the gods and their ancestors.

The Incas believed in the saying: "As above, so below." So, when they saw the shift in the stars, they were likely to mourn and eventually accept their fate as a destitute civilization.

Pachacuti, the Inca ruler who reversed the equation

However, one Inca ruler chose life instead. He thought of a radical idea that no one had thought of before. If the events that took place on Earth resembled those of the Heavens, then the reverse must also be true.

Spurred on by another astrological phenomenon (a unique conjecture between the planets Saturn and Jupiter that, according to Dr. Williams, could have been interpreted as the creator god Viracocha handing power to Pachacuti), he began an era of conquest. Within three generations the Inca dominion would expand massively, covering almost the entire Western region of South America.

But what could have been at the heart of his success? Dr. Williams believes that Pachacuti had a unique mission - to have a chance at reversing the prophecy, he would need to work hard to reunite the 12 original tribes of the creation myth who had suffered a great deal in the 800-year-long civil war. This, he believes, would have proved to the gods that they deserved a second chance.

The role of children sacrifice

Just like it's difficult for our modern minds to grasp the effect of the constellations on the Ancient Inca, it is even more difficult to understand how such a sophisticated culture could have exercised the gruesome rite of child sacrifice. Such a horrid act cannot be justified - we can only attempt to understand the motivations behind it, lest we run the risk of reducing the Inca to nothing more but savage beasts.

The Inca believed that, just like the 12 tribes had come from the stars, so did every human. And after they died, each one of them would return to their heavenly home once again. Dr. Williams believes the sincerity of their mission to overcome the prophecy could only be measured by the extent of that which they were willing to sacrifice. What higher price could a nation pay than the sacrifice of its offspring?

The Inca believed the children would act as messengers who would deliver their plea to the gods when they returned to their celestial bodies. This is why they picked two children from each tribe so that each heavenly deity would be spoken to.

How did the Incas expand their Empire?

The Incas, especially their emperor Pachacuti, had a strong desire or motivation for expanding their Empire to the extent that they did - if we take Dr. William Sullivan's view, then they did this in an effort to reverse the prophecy of their empire that the Incas had seen in their celestial bodies. But how did they practically win over such a vast area of land, people and tribes?

Diplomacy

Although they were no stranger to warfare, the Incas always began their conquests by diplomatic means. They negotiated with the local rulers and bribed them by promising good posts and rich rewards, if they cooperated. Their early imperial success owes much to building strong alliances, conscripting defeated enemies into their own army and confronting small target societies and tribes with an overwhelming force - without actually fighting them. Once they achieved their desired effect of overwhelming a target society, the Inca messengers offered them favorable terms of surrender: elites received gifts and could keep their status in society while communities could keep many of their resources and customs. Thus, many of the societies that the Incas targeted were simultaneously charmed and frightened into surrender.

Fortifications

As the years went by, the Incas shifted their attention from small-scale victories to imperial domination. The larger the empire grew, the more resources they needed to rage a war. To save their resources, the Incas built a network of internal garrisons, frontier fonts and systems of roads, with storage depots and support facilities for the army. The Incas also resettled restive people and fortified hot spots, in particular.

Still, there were few fortified strongholds, except in the hostile Northern Ecuador and the southeastern frontier. There's an especially high concentration of Inca forts near Quito, especially at Pambamarca. The purpose of these was to deter raids or cut them off from behind, rather than deflect or defeat potential attacks from outside enemy forces.

Strategy and logistics

Even when it came to fighting a battle, the Incas were master planners and owed much of their success to excellent strategy and logistics, rather than training of their soldiers, battle tactics or technology. The Incas were at their best preparing for a battle, and, as the Inca empire grew, the emperor himself was in charge of strategic planning. The different ethnic groups that made up the Inca army were led by their own lords.

As they travelled to the designated battlefield, the vast armies camped in tents, supported by provincial centres along the main roads that could assist the soldiers and provide resources for them. An array of storehouses supported the soldiers with food, arms, clothing, and other items. The only transport was llama caravans - otherwise the soldiers and their kin travelled on foot.

Battle tactics

The actual battles were either great melees on open terrain or assaults on fortified strongholds. The Incas also employed feigned withdrawals paired with pincer counterattacks and flanking maneuvers. The victories were grandly celebrated, and the Inca emperor usually tread on their enemy's head in the Golden Enclosure or the main plaza in Cuzco. Others made drinking cups out of the heads of their enemies, or flayed the skin of their enemies and used them to make drums that were played during ceremonial events in Cuzco. Soldiers who'd been particularly courageous and displayed valour were richly rewarded - however, the nobles received greater gifts than the commoners, in accordance to the class structure in the Inca society.

Chapter 7 – Social Order in the Inca Society

The Inca society was built around several complex social rites and rituals, and no one was exempt from carrying these out. That included the nobles and the ruler.

How the Inca state was governed

The Incas called their large empire by the name of *Tawantinsuyu*. Translated from their language Quechua, it means 'The Four Parts Together.' These four parts were called the *Suyu*, and each one was governed by *Apu* who was a great lord. These *suyus* were split into two sectors - the upper sector and the lower sector, in line with the Inca notion of duality.

The upper sector:

- *Chinchaysuyu*
  This area occupied most of highland Peru and Ecuador in the north, as well as the coastal areas. This was the most prestigious part and the most populous one.

- *Antisuyu*
  Spreading northeast, this area contained the eastern jungles and the slopes of the Andean mountains.

The lower sector:

- *Kollasuyu*
  This was the largest yet least densely populated part of the empire, spreading across the south-east. This area included southeastern Peru, highland Bolivia and the northern part of Chile, as well as some of the northwest Argentina. This region was named after the Coya ethnic group who lived on the shores of Lake Titicaca.

- *Cuntisuyu*
  This was the smallest region of the empire, occupying the southwest area of the empire, spreading from Cuzco to the southern coast of Peru.

These four quarters of the empire were mirrored in the capital city of Cuzco in the way it was constructed.

The role of social norms in keeping the empire together

To keep such a vast and varied empire together, a competent military force was insufficient. A strict governing structure was also required. This meant every member of the society had to comply with strict social norms and religious rite.

When discussing the social obligations and duties of the various people and casts that made up the Inca society, we once again come up against the unreliability of certain popular historical sources. According to the chronicler Garcilaso de la Vega - an omnipotent emperor governed over a vast and complicated bureaucratic system that included local rulers and governing bodies. However, de la Vega was interested in presenting his ancestors as benevolent monarchs. The opinions that most of the Spanish chroniclers collected were those of the aristocracy, meaning that they were skewed in the favour of the ruling class and peppered with propaganda.

Although some societies that the Inca incorporated into their empire did eventually adapt their customs, many did not and simply carried on with their own religious and social rites whenever they could. They paid their taxes diligently, however the Inca rule went skin-deep and the locals were never fully converted to the Inca belief and social system. Since there were only about 100.000 Inca that ruled over an empire of almost ten million, most of the locals never actually saw a real Inca in their life, and there were hundreds of these smaller individual societies within the Inca empire.

However, there were rules that everyone obeyed, and the king and his wife were no exception to these.

The king and queen

Following the death of a ruler, his inheritance was split into two parts - the most able son inherited the ruling power while his kinship inherited all the king's properties.

The King was an absolute monarch, the divine being of god's representation on Earth. He was the military leader, the head of all the different social groups and the political leader, as well as provided sacred leadership. At least that's the idea that was perpetuated across the Inca empire. The reality was quite different -

the King was constantly torn between pleasing the various aristocratic groups that existed, to make sure that he was recognised as the legitimate successor to a deceased monarch and remained in power until the day he died.

The rulers were advised, counselled and even assassinated by their relatives. Thus, only the king's ideal was omnipotent - in practice, they had to manoeuvre among the different interests and needs of their relatives, lest they are torn from power.

The king had different 'duties' he had to perform during various stages of his life, and not all kings could carry them out successfully. When a new Inca ruler came to power - although he was considered omnipotent and god's representation on Earth - he still had to prove himself as worthy of the title first. This was usually achieved by military means - the Inca rulers had to establish their supreme power by success in military conflict, and win favour with the aristocracy. Once he'd succeeded to impress them, he was anointed as a deity who was supreme among all the other people who walked upon the Earth. While military valour was important, so was the king's sanctity and generosity. Every four days, the king had a duty of provisioning the population of Cuzco with food from the royal store houses.

During the day, the king conversed with the living as well as the dead, eating and drinking with them, before retiring for the night in his palace. When he was granted his title, he assumed a new name that was given to him.

Ritual pomp and feasting comprised the daily routine of a king - from early morning through to late night, the king had to entertain his guests from both upper and lower parts of Cuzco and watch over the regular feasting in Cuzco's central plaza. His guests had to obey certain norms, too. Anyone who approached the emperor had to show their humility by taking off their shoes and loading their back with a small bundle that was a symbol for a burden to carry. When the ruler received visitors or conducted political affairs, he spoke through a screen via an interpreter.

The king's outfit

The Emperor had just as many elaborate costumes as he had rituals and duties.

- Headband of braided cloth sometimes adorned with feathers. The king's crown was a braided cloth that had a fringe that dangled before the ruler's eyes.
- Large ear spools that marked the king's social status and prestige, and were worn by the aristocrats. The Spanish called 'pig ears.'
- A staff, covered in tiny feathers and three larger feathers that projected from the tip of the staff. Used during ritual processions to represent the ruler's power.
- A golden mace and royal stand made of cloth that was painted until it stood stiff.

The installation and death of a ruler

During such events, all of the participants of the royal families of Cuzco gathered in the central plaza to celebrate. The statues of the sun and other main gods were present, as well as representatives of all the important shrines.

During the installation of an emperor, some 200 children aged 4 to 10 were sacrificed, adorned with golden jewelled items, sea shells and statues. The death of a ruler also saw the ritual of human sacrifice, including children, although the number of exactly how many were executed is unclear. The Incas saw children as the purest human beings that gave them a special sacrificial status, and the ones chosen for sacrifice had to be particularly physically healthy.

The sacrifice of children was a long affair, and it did not take place in the same plaza as the celebrations. Months or sometimes even years before the event, the children were fed with elite diets, consisting of maize and animal proteins. When the day of the sacrifice drew nearer, they were dressed in expensive clothes and adorned with jewels, ready for their sacred pilgrimage to Cuzco, where they met the emperor who held a feast to honour the children.

The priests then took the children on a long and arduous journey to a sacred burial site on a high mountaintop. There, children were given an intoxicating drink that minimized both their pain and resistance. The priests then killed the children by strangulation or a heavy blow to the head. The less fortunate ones were left out in the extreme cold until they lost consciousness and died.

The emperor Pachacuti had a special ceremony carried out after his death per his request. He instructed people to mourn for an entire year and to carry his body to all the important sights and places where he'd won great victories while people cheered on.

2,000 llamas were sacrificed in Cuzco in Pachacuti's memory, along with another thousand llamas that were sacrificed all over the empire. Children, too, formed part of the sacrifice.

The king's principal wife

The coupling of the king and his principal wife was not a simple affair. While the women associated with the king (his wife and his mother) could enjoy priviledges, they also had unique duties they had to perform, and they were subject to as much danger as the king himself if he were overthrown. In line with the Inca notion of duality, the king and his principal wife formed a perfect union.

Tupa Inca Yupanki, the second Inca ruler, began the tradition of marrying his sister and being coronated together as a married couple. This was always the sister from the same father, but she may have had a different mother. Although this idea may seem abhorrent to us, it did reduce bloodshed and the number of claims that could be made for the throne during the Inca civilization. The principal wife had her line of duties to perform. She was seen as *coya* (or queen) and as the mother of the nation.

Before she could become a *coya,* the queen had to meet certain standards. She had to have pure Inca blood flowing in her veins. She had to be the king's sister or one of his first cousins. She had some independent power, and she could act as a persuasive political advisor to her husband and his succeeding son. Traditionally, it was the woman's role to promote a selected son as the royal successor. The mother was crucial because the rulers did not belong to a particular kin group but founded their own, closely identified to that of their mother's.

The wife was the liaison between the ruler's relatives and the king. The mother of the king held a influence, and she was just as influential after death as she had been while she was alive. This was done through a medium or an interpreter who spoke on behalf of an image or a mummy of a deceased queen.

But women associated with the king (like his wife or mother) did not only enjoy privileges - they also encountered certain dangers when a change of politics occurred. For example, if a king was overthrown in a coup, he may have been spared but his mother would not. A good example of this was the defeat of Vascar by Arualpa - when he was defeated, Vascar, his wife, and his mother were taken as prisoners, while others associated with the king were pardoned.

What's interesting is that the queen's influence increased when she became a mother to the next ruler, and her power continued even after her death. The king's wife or mother was an important advisory.

The king's other wives

The king had many consorts and princesses of royal blood who were his secondary wives. To illustrate just how many different wives a single ruler could have, the last undisputed Inca ruler Huayna Capac took 2,000 of them on the way to his military conquests in Ecuador. His other 4,000 wives were left behind in Cuzco.

The *panaqa*

The *panaqa* was the most exalted kin group at the time of the Spanish arrival. According to the Inca customs, they inherited all the deceased king's properties. However, they had a price to pay - they had to execute all the rituals surrounding the deceased ruler's mummy and perform elaborate ancestor worship rituals.

At the time of the Spanish arrival in 1532, there were ten *panaqa* or ten noble Inca kin groups, who were distant relatives of the royalty. The kin groups in Cuzco were made up of different ethnic groups who had lived in the region when the founding fathers arrived.

Each *panaqa* kin group was formed of descendants of an Inca ruler. The first five of these *panaqas* formed the lower part of Cuzco, and the latter formed the upper Cuzco. Thus, the descent groups who were related to the first five Inca rulers were less influential than the most recent five.

The *panaqa* could nonetheless influence the decisions about who the next ruler should be. Therefore, the kings and the various kin groups were involved in constant power negotiations. It was good news if the king the *panaqas* selected was successful in their claim, and bad news if he was not. For instance, after his victory and return to Cuzco, Arualpa's forces wiped out all the *panaqa* kin groups who'd formed allegiance and supported Vascar. This means the most recent five *panaqa* kin groups were slain, with only few managing to escape and later making a claim to the Spanish king to restore them back to their resources.

Ancestor worship

The Inca's rigid social structure and the division of roles incorporated the living, as well as the dead. This is because the Incas believed the world was divided between the living, the dead, the gods and the spirits and each had their duties to perform. Ancestors were venerated, and they had their duties to perform. Mummies of aristocrats participated in the day-to-day political decision-making and elaborate rituals.

For example, the mummies were brought out daily into the main square to participate in the affairs of the state. The male and female attendants ate and drank on behalf of the mummies. They also made firewood and burned fires in front of each mummy.

The attendants brought all the food they ate and put them in front of the mummies; they then burned in the fires.

Large images of gold, silver, and clay were also placed in front of these mummies, and chicha was poured out for the mummies to drink.

The real mummies only 'attended' the most important rituals. Where participation was not paramount, effigies of the mummies or 'brother images' were sent in their place. The mummies also visited their living relatives, and they weighed so little that they could be carried from place to place on a man's shoulders.

According to the chronicler Pachacuti Yanki, Vascar who raged war against Arualpa asserted his belonging to a royal kinship by having his mother marry his father's mummy. This served to affirm his belonging to the royal bloodline.

What's most peculiar about these tales is that was involved in decision-making, when the living could not agree. Thus, it was more than just a symbolism that the mummies participated in the political decisions.

The Inca aristocrats were masters at manipulating their history for political gain. For example, one family would tell the tales that only represented their lineage in a good light. There wasn't much weight given to the truth - everyone had their version of history.

The life of a local and military service

From birth to death, the local people had to follow specific social rules and rituals. This included military service. At certain times during the year, when they did not have to harvest their crops, the men from different provinces and ethnic groups were summoned to join the Inca military service as a way of paying their tax. There were no means of transport during the Inca days, so many of the soldiers came on foot, dragging their entire families with them (since the military conquests could last a long time). Many died during battles, and it wasn't unusual to see each soldier bringing with him twice as many followers.

The Inca fights were truly spectacular affairs, but the Incas only resorted to these, if they had not managed to succumb an ethnic group or settlement with gifts and bribes. Although the fights were often bloodied and brutal, each soldier dressed in their best garments. Certain ethnic groups wore their costumes, so it was easier to tell during a battle who was a friend and who was a foe. This gave an eerie sense of beauty to the brutal spectacle.

Chapter 8 – The Different Roles of Women in the Inca Society

The Inca believed in the concept of duality.

They also believed other things in life came in pairs. Just like the Moon was not complete without the Sun, and the tears of the Moon were silver while the sweat of the Sun was gold, so a male was not complete without a female. Although women adapted many different roles in the Inca society, they were highly valued and played their role as much within married life, as within the religious ceremonies and advancing political agendas.

Women from ethnic minorities

Many ethnic groups existed within the Inca Empire, and they had their social norms and structures. Many of these underwent significant changes when they were conquered by the Incas.

For example, Christine Hastorf had researched an ethnic group called Wanka who still exist in the Junín Region of modern central Peru and fought fiercely before they were assimilated into the Inca Empire.

Before the assimilation, their households appeared to have been autonomous, socio-economic units. People ate a diet that consisted largely of potatoes, although there has been evidence found to suggest communities of women did process some maize crops in their diet. Nonetheless, the domestic and roles within the community seemed to have been split equally among men and women - the skeletons found in archaeological digs show they ate a diet of similar items at similar percentages. This complementary view of gender aligns with the Inca ideals of duality that may have existed in the rest of the Andean society.

However, things changed after the conquest. The Incas imposed their government upon the Wanka people. From 1460 to 1532 AD the Wanka consumed a lot more corn and almost no potatoes. The households had less freedom now, and this impacted women.

More of the Wanka men became labourers, drafted into the government's work parties who probably used food, particularly meat, and drink as a reward. The role of women degraded, and they were even excluded from important state rituals.

Married women

There was a clear division between married life for the lower classes and married life for the upper classes - namely, in the number of wives a husband could have. The lower classes tended to have monogamous relationships for the simple fact they were unable to support more than one wife and all her children.

In lower class monogamous marriages, women were somewhat more valued. Even before the Incas arrived, many ethnic groups in the Andean vicinity, held the belief that the roles of men and women were complementary and interdependent. The married couple worked as a team. Women were responsible for cooking, looking after children and weaving while men carried out more physical labour. In fact, women had to pay tribute to the state by means of producing a certain number of textiles.

Men from the upper class valued women less. Their wives often came from the *Acllahuasi* or the house of The Chosen Women.

The Chosen Women

The women who were admitted to the *Acllahuasi* became the most educated women in the entire Inca Empire. How did they get in?

As the name suggests, they were chosen by the government officials. Each year, the most good-looking eight to ten-year-old girls from each town were conscripted to enter the *Acllahuasi* by specially elected officials called *Apu Panaca* or 'Lord of the Sisters'.

To be chosen was particularly good news for women from the lower classes, as it allowed them to move upward in society. But not all of them were so lucky. After spending four years in complete chastity studying in the capital city of Cuzco, the women had different fates.

Though it may have been beautifully presented, the idea of the *Acllahuasi* was to fully remove the women from their homes and duties there, so they could entirely devote themselves to the service of the state - mind, body, and soul.

The Chosen Women were instructed by *mamaconas* or teachers in various trades, such as religious rites, secret knowledge, the preparation of sacred foods and the elaboration of fine fabrics. Since clothes were among the most precious gifts the Inca could give to those they favoured, along with cocoa and beautiful women, all the women in these convents learned how to make textiles. They also learned how to brew an important corn drink called chicha.

While some women learned valuable trades, others were less lucky. The best-looking girls, in fact, were chosen for sacrifice to the gods. Others were assigned to become concubines for the Emperor or wives of other important men the ruler wanted to ally or honour. Others still stayed permanently at the *Acllahuasi*, becoming the next generation of *mamaconas*. The upper-class women usually completed administrative tasks while the lower-class women carried out work that involved more manual labour.

There was one important restriction for all of them - these women had to remain chaste for the rest of their lives. If they were found to be pregnant, the woman and her lover were buried alive, according to the laws and customs. This was rarely a problem though since no man could enter the *Acllahuasi* or speak to one of the virgin priestesses.

Women at work

What were the other typical roles of women in the Inca society? While weaving was a woman's profession, they also worked in weaving shops that were owned and overseen by men.

Some women became prostitutes and lived in houses overseen by a supervisor. Although these women were social outcasts who were not allowed to have any contact with non-prostitutes, their supervisor was paid by the government.

Women also became healers and midwives. Some of them even induced abortions.

Conclusion

Although one could argue that overall women were not as highly valued as men in the Inca society, they did carry out some very important tasks behind the scenes.

Within married life, a woman was an indispensable companion to her husband, at least within the domestic structure of the lower classes. Within upper-class marriages, women played an essential role in advancing politics through diplomatic marriage. And within the broader context of society, women were almost solely responsible for running the textile industry, around which the economy revolved.

Women played a crucial, yet somewhat passive rule in Inca society.

Chapter 9 – Inca Religious Order and Ideology

Tradition, politics, and beliefs all served as ingredients to create a potent mix of Inca ideology that served to help them claim supremacy over other cultures.

Incas believed they shared the Universe with the gods, deities and nature spirits, all who needed to be venerated. Just like the Earth was filled with living creatures and spirits, the sky too was filled with animals and gods.

The official state ideology justified the Inca supremacy. The chief god within the Inca pantheon of deities was the Sun god Inti, and the Inca ruler was considered Inti's son.

The cult of the Sun god Inti

Although many other Andean societies held the Moon in much higher esteem, the Incas venerated the Sun god Inti. By 1532 when the Spanish first contacted the Inca civilization, they noted Inti worship outshone all the other deities combined. The Sun was incredibly important - not only because of the role it played in sustaining nature but also for its symbolic meaning for the Inca civilization.

Because the Incas claimed their ruler was the son of the actual Sun god Inti, their ruler could claim supremacy in the natural order of things. He was the son of the most important celestial body, and therefore the Inca society was superior to others. The Incas believed a reverence for the Inca ruler was reverence for the Universe itself. They thought they, as a nation, were vital to the world's well-being.

There were two primary visions or representations of the Sun god Inti, as accounted for in various chronicles:

- A small figurine of a boy named 'punchao' (or 'day').

  Solar rays projected from his head and he wore large ear spools, a chest ornament, and a royal head band. Serpents and lions projected out from his body. And he had a somewhat more gruesome attribute, too. The vital organs of the deceased rulers were burned to ash and then inserted into his abdomen so that he could bridge the gap between the divine beings and humanity. In 1572 when the last Inca ruler was executed by the Spanish conquistadors, the idol of 'punchao' that had gone missing for a long time somewhere in the jungle, was recovered. However, it was lost again shortly afterward.

- A more traditional solar disk.

  As opposed to the *punchao* figurine, sources disagree as to whether the solar disk was an authentic Inca invention. It may have been a Spanish invention that was passed down to the Incas. Over the years, as the Spanish and Inca traditions blurred, the solar disk may have been presented as an Inca invention.

The High Priest of the Sun or Inti was usually one of the Inca ruler's close relatives. However, there were some exceptions. The ruler Huayna Capac, for example, took on the role of the High Priest for himself to dispose of a potential threat such a person could cause him.

The importance of the cult of the Sun god could also be seen in the types of buildings that were constructed to Inti. The religious complex of Coricancha or the Golden Enclosure within Cuzco contained the Temple of the Sun that the Inca considered to be at the very centre of the world, and one of its most sacred sites.

The cult of the Sun god generated pretty good income for the state. Every province was supposed to dedicate goods and crops to the Sun, and so there were large storehouses, herds, and staff who were all committed to the church's holdings.

Aside from Inti, there were other deities who were highly esteemed in the Inca religion - Viracocha, the Creator God whom we have already discussed and the moon goddess Quilla (or Mother Moon).

Mother Moon

Quilla or Mother Moon was the wife of the Sun god Inti. Echoing the Inca notions of duality and complementary natures of males and females, Quilal enjoyed similar privileges to the Sun god. Silver was her colour, as opposed to Inti's gold. To the Incas, she was particularly important in calculating time and their annual cycles, many of which were based on the lunar cycle. She was also revered as the deity responsible for regulating the female menstrual cycle.

Beautiful tales surround the other deities within the Inca pantheon, so let's take a brief look at some of them.

Apu Illapu

He was the god of rain and important in agriculture. When people needed rain for their crops, they would turn to Apu Illapu for help. They also believed he drew his water from the Milky Way before he poured it down on earth.

Ayar Cachi

Ayar Cachi was among the first couples that feature in the Creation myth, and set on his way towards Cuzco along with the others. However, his temper was so hot the first Inca ruler Manco Capac decided to lock him up in the same cave he'd come from. The cave is situated some 30km from Cuzco, and the locals believe he's the one causing earthquakes in the area, as he attempts to set himself free.

Pachamama

She was the wife of the Creator God Viracocha (also known as Pachacamac). She was worshipped as the earth goddess or earth mother, a tradition that still exists in the tribes who live in the Andean mountains. People there make offerings to Pachamama in the form of cocoa leaves and *chicha* beer. She is usually worshipped during major agricultural events and occasions.

Sach'amama and K'uychi

These two deities form another illustration of the Inca notion of duality and complimentary natures of the male and female roles. Sach'amama was a feminine deity, also known as Mother Tree. She was depicted as a two-headed snake. However, when she passed on to the heavenly realm, she was transformed into a different deity - K'uychi.

K'uychi was the masculine expression of Sach'amama. He was the rainbow god, associated with fertility.

Despite the mostly complimentary and harmonious natures of the deities, there was sometimes competition among them and their worshippers on earth. Human sacrifice was one manifestation of this contest.

The role of human sacrifice

Although the extent of human sacrifices within the Inca civilization never reached the vast numbers of victims the Aztecs executed as part of their religious rites (believed to be as many as 80,000 during especially important events), the Incas did participate in significant numbers of human sacrifice.

A maximum of 2,000 – 3,000 victims could be executed at any one time as part of the human sacrifice tradition, but many of the religious sacrifices involved llamas or special goods rather than humans. Nonetheless, children were usually among the victims.

The archaeologist, Steve Borget made an astonishing discovery in 1996, while digging near the Moche site. There, he found over 70 remains of dismembered sacrificial victims. What's more, he discovered many of them were sacrificed during periods of heavy rainfall - such periods could be dangerous to the Andean cultures, so it makes sense the Incas conducted religious rites and offered sacrifices to appease their gods during this time.

In fact, human sacrifice was usually done to control the nature and change the mind of the god's. During the Inca rulers, Pachacuti's reign who made a stand to reverse the prophecy that predicted the Inca reign was coming to an end, thousands of llamas were sacrificed each year, during the December solstice. Once the llamas had been killed, the high priests put their blood into tiny jars made of clay and distributed these across the Inca Empire.

Children were also sacrificed during Pachacuti's reign. Usually on mountaintops and at major shrines that belonged to each lineage, with the intention, the children would return to the stars to deliver a message to spare the Inca empire from the prophecy that predicted its downfall.

Annual ceremonies in Cuzco

The annual cycle of ceremonies in Cuzco were all shaped according to the heavens. The Incas were very knowleadgable about the celestial bodies and their movements. This was particularly evident when it came to celebrating the Winter and Summer solstice, events that were accurately predicted. Many of the annual celebrations were also centred around the appearance of the New Moon.

There were two calendars in the Inca system that regulated the annual cycles of worship and celebration - a solar calendar that consisted of 365 days and a lunar calendar that consisted of 28.5-day cycles. There is an 11-day disparity between the two calendars over a year.

Nonetheless, the two calendars led to an elaborate cycle of annual festivities.

The *Inti Raymi* or the Sun Festival (the Summer Solstice)

Translated from Quechua, the name means the Sun Celebration. Today, the festival is celebrated on the 24th of June in Cuzco's Fortress of Sacsayhuaman. According to the Spanish chronicler Garcilazo de la Vega, *Inti Raymi* celebration was one of the most important annual celebrations across the entire Inca Empire. The celebrations lasted for nine days in Cuzco's central plaza.

Only the Sapa Inca, the nobility, and the Inca army could participate in these celebrations, along with the effigies of dead rulers and aristocrats. But it wasn't all fun and games. Three days before the celebrations, the participants had to go through a period of purification. They could only eat white maize and a certain herb known as *chucham* during this period.

On June 24th, the Sapa Inca would take his place on a stage in front of the pilgrims and drink a maize-based rink called *chicha de jora*, honouring the Sun god Inti. Dances, shells and musical instruments accompanied the celebrations. It was a colourful affair too - both men and women painted their faces yellow, wearing deer heads and using their antlers as musical instruments. Women would toss an array of red flowers and colourful feathers at the Inca ruler as he returned to his palace.

There was a darker side to the celebrations, too. The chronicler Juan Betanzos accounts that children under ten years of age were brought to Cuzco to be sacrificed. Black llamas suffered a similar fate, being cut open with a ceremonial knife. Their organs were later used to predict the future.

The Queen's Festival (August)

During the month of the Queen's festival, the purification ritual or *citua* was performed. The ceremony took place during the rainy season when people were prone to fall ill, as a way of purifying themselves and their city and guarding against disease.

Cuzco's residents engaged in some bizarre yet seemingly fun activities to open the festival - they struck each other with torches and shook clothing outside their doorways to purify themselves and 'shake out' negativity and malice.

Usually, the principal men involved in these festivities met together each year to decide how the ceremony would be carried out. Lots of activities took place in Cuzco and the surrounding areas.

To begin, the Incas summoned some warriors who were to stand at the entrance of their main temples, as though they were ready to fight. To defend the city against disease, all seemingly 'sketchy types' had to be expelled from its walls. This included all foreigners and people born with some form of physical deformity. Even dogs suffered and were thrown out due to their howling.

The warriors assembled in the city's main square where they were split into four groups of 100 men. Each group marched in a different direction, to extend the ritual of purification across the whole kingdom. They shouted: 'Get out, disease!' and marched several miles beyond the city.

The Inca and the principal people involved in these ceremonies danced all night, followed by bathing themselves, their clothes and weapons in the rivers and lakes that surrounded the city. They believed by doing this, they let the disease flow out and into the sea. People also fasted as a form of purification, and, just like pilgrims take on sacred journeys today, the Andean people visited sacred sites and shrines where they believed their tribe or kin group to have originated.

Eclipses and Movements of Comets

The Andean people were unable to predict Solar and Lunar eclipses, and, as opposed to other Mesoamerican civilizations like the Maya or the Aztecs, the Incas were frightened of these events. When a Solar eclipse occurred, the Incas consulted the oracles. One of the explanations the oracles provided was that the Inca ruler or a great prince was about to die and thus the Sun had gone into mourning. In response, the Incas fasted, sacrificed animals, and even innocent boys and girls, to appease the gods.

When it came to a Lunar eclipse, the Incas usually believed that a puma or a snake was eating the Moon. To correct this natural sequence of events, the Incas would act as loudly as they could. They beat drums and shouted, whipped dogs until they howled, threw weapons and spears at the moon and did everything they possibly could to frighten the beast away.

The Incas also told future by the movement of comets. For example, the last Inca leader Atahualpa predicted his death when he saw a great comet flash across the skies as he was imprisoned by the Spanish conquistadors.

The role of other Andean religions

Naturally, when ruling over such a vast Empire, the Incas encountered other tribal religions and rites. How did they deal with them? They either incorporated the deities (such as Pachamama) into their pantheon of gods or exploited the religious beliefs and traditions of other cultures for their own political gain.

Each local group in the Andes had their own beliefs and rites. Most of the local tribes did have one common religious feature though, and that was ancestor worship.

Most of the Andean societies worshipped their ancestors. They also knew of a special place (a cave or a natural formation) they believed to have been the place of origin for their society.

This was good news for the Incas who used the religious rites of other local societies to their advantage. For example, they held ancestral mummies of other tribes as hostages in Cuzco to force the locals to come and reclaim them, so they could once again pay homage to them. The Incas went as far as to publicly whip these mummies, until the local people they were trying to subjugate finally gave into them.

But when it came to oracles who could foretell the future, things were different. Allegedly, thousands of oracles existed within most of the Andean societies. Some of these oracles were older than the societies themselves, stretching back thousands of years. The Incas incorporated these oracles into their religion, continuing to consult the same oracles as the societies that existed before them. For example, a notable coastal oracle was Pachacamac whom the local communities had been consulting for at least two thousand years.

Chapter 10 – Tour of the Greatest Inca Sights

The environment of the area that used to be the ancient Inca Empire is truly spectacular. If you take a road trip from Lima, the central coast of Peru and travel about 200km East, you would be starting your journey from the desert coast, passing through a mountain range and its snow-topped peaks, and eventually, end up in the Amazonian tropical rain forest. The Inca Empire included 20 of the world's 34 major life zones, and you would pass from one to the next in within an hour of walking.

This naturally affected how the Incas built their homes and used their environment.

How the Incas constructed their homes

With such a vast mountain range covering a considerable portion of their empire, the Incas naturally constructed their homes high up, many miles above the sea level. About two-thirds of the population, in fact, lived some 3,300m above sea level. This also affected the way the locals could overcome the problem of high altitude, the Incas invented terrace farming. They built steps of land for agriculture down the mountainside, and this helped them to create flat lands even in the mountains. They also had a good irrigation system - the Incas could channel the rainwater through each step of the terraced lands. They also constructed aqueducts that helped them carry the water more efficiently to wherever it was needed.

Although this view may come from the Inca propaganda at the time, it is believed no one went hungry in the Inca empire. The common people may have eaten little meat, compared to the nobles, but everyone was well fed.

In fact, the Inca were the first society to grow potatoes, along with many other crops, such as corn and quinoa. These were the three staple crops of the Inca civilization, and the latter helped them to make many different dishes. These include flour, soups, and cereal. The Incas also ate a great variety of other fruit and crop - tomatoes, avocados, peppers, strawberries, peanuts, squash, sweet potatoes, beans, pineapple, bananas, spices. They also favoured coco leaves to make their chocolate drinks. They were no stranger to the sweeter things in life either as they kept honeybees.

According to some sources, the Inca grew so much food it had to be dried and kept in specially constructed storage buildings.

Due to the high altitudes, the climate was colder than on the mainland, and therefore better suited for storing food. So, the Incas put the food outside to freeze and stamped on it until all the water had gone. To finish the drying process, they left it out in the sun for a while.

Most notable Inca sacred sites

Many of the most impressive Inca religious sites are still visited today. Since everything in the Inca empire was tied up with their religious practices, many of these sites have been built according to the Inca sacred geometry.

Macchu Piccu

Macchu Piccu.

https://commons.wikimedia.org/wiki/File:Peru_Machu_Picchu_Sunrise_2.jpg

On the top of the list for any tourist setting out to discover the Inca legacy is the stunning site of Macchu Piccu. The ruins of their great temples at Macchu Piccu were rediscovered by a Hawaiian historian Hiram in 1911 after many centuries of total secrecy. The locals knew about the ruins that were located above the Urubamba Valley. But since they were completely invisible from below, the locals were cautious of sharing their coordinates. It was self-contained, as the site was surrounded by agricultural terraces and natural springs where the locals could get water.

Ollantaytambo

Ollantaytambo

https://commons.wikimedia.org/wiki/File:Ollantaytambo_terraces.jpg

Many tourists nowadays start the Inca Trail in Ollantaytambo and make their way to Maccu Picchu over several days of walking. Ollantaytambo was the royal estate that belonged to the Inca Emperor Pachacuti. He conquered the region and served as a stronghold of Inca resistance during the Spanish conquest.

Choquequirao

The main structures of Choquequirao by Bryan Dougherty

Bryan Dougherty (bryand_nyc) from New York City, USA, CC BY-SA 2.0 <https://creativecommons.org/licenses/by-sa/2.0>, via Wikimedia Commons
https://commons.wikimedia.org/wiki/File:Choquequirao.jpg

Translated, Choquequirao means 'the Cradle of Gold' and indeed, set in its breathtaking valley; it could be considered to be just that! Like many of the Inca sites, Choquequirao is located at 3,085m above sea level. There is a staircase configuration, made of 180 terraces. Choquequirao is much larger than Machu Picchu and built in a remarkably different style. It is less frequented than Machu Picchu too since access can be a problem.

Inca Pisac

Pisac

https://commons.wikimedia.org/wiki/File:Pisac006.jpg

Translated, Pisac means 'partridge' and this sacred site was indeed built in the shape of a bird, matching their bird constellations. Where now are only ruins, there was once a military citadel, a complex of religious temples and individual houses. This area overlooks the Sacred Valley, and it is believed this site helped defend the southern entrance to the Valley, connecting the Inca Empire with the borders of the surrounding rainforest.

The Temple of the Sun

Old Coricancha

https://commons.wikimedia.org/wiki/File:OldCoricancha.jpg

Coricancha (or the Temple of the Sun) was the crowning jewel of the Incas capital of Cuzco. The city was located in the shape of a Puma, and the Temple was believed to be its tail. It was the holiest of all sights in the Incan mythology. The Temple's construction began sometime in the 1200 AD, using a particular masonry style that was a signature for the Incas.

The Temple was not only well constructed but also located in a point of geographical importance - it was built in the very centre of four main highways that led out to the four districts of the empire. Thus, it symbolised the center stage that religion played within the Inca Empire. It was a grand building, housing over 4,000 priests and the building also functioned as a calendar. According to Drew Reed who writes for The Guardian: "Shadows cast by stones placed on the foothills could be seen from the temple, marking out the solstice and equinoxes observed by the Incan empire."

Much of the temple was destroyed by the Spanish conquistadors, who melted down much of its gold adornments. They built their cathedral on top of this sacred site, maintaining the original stone foundations. An earthquake destroyed the cathedral a few hundred years later, while its Incan foundations remained intact. Today, it is open and frequented by tourists who visit Cuzco every year.

Chapter 11 - From Pachacuti to the Arrival of the Spanish

Túpac Inca Yupanqui (c. 1471–1493 AD)

This Inca ruler was known as the 'noble Inca accountant.' He was the legitimate successor of Pachacuti who left a vast Empire in his hands. Back in 1463, Túpac Inca Yupanqui had proven his valour when his father appointed him to head the Inca army. He succeeded as a ruler too, expanding the Empire by adding lands northward along the Andes through to modern Ecuador. In fact, he became very fond of Quito, a city in Ecuador. Túpac Inca Yupanqui rebuilt it with architects brought in from Cuzco.

And he didn't stop there. He subdued the Collas and conquered a province known as Antis. He also built a large fortress on the plateau above Cuzco that held storehouses of food and clothing. He also imposed new rules and taxes, appointing two new Governor Generals. He was quite the ladies' man too, leaving behind him 90 illegitimate children and only two legitimate sons. The son Ccapac Huari whom he'd named as his successor was killed soon after his death, clearing the way for his son Titu Cusi Hualpa to become the next emperor.

Huayna Capac (c. 1493–1527 AD)

After his coronation, Titu Cusi Hualpa took on the name of Huayna Capac or 'the young mighty one.' He had no legitimate sons with his principal queen and sister Coya Cusirimay. However, his second royal wife Araua Ocllo gave birth to several sons, including the contender for the throne Huáscar, who'd be engaged in a vicious civil war with his half-brother Atahualpa during the arrival of the Spanish.

Huayna Capac continued with the expansion of the Inca Empire, subduing many tribes in present-day Chile and Argentina, and conquering territories as far north as Ecuador and the south of Colombia. For political gains, he married the Quito Queen Paccha Duchicela Shyris XVI to subdue the Kingdom of Quito in modern-day Ecuador into the Inca Empire. Atahualpa was born of this marriage, and would later battle Huáscar for the throne.

Similarly to his predecessor Túpac Inca Yupanqui, Huayna Capac was also very fond of Ecuador. He built cities there, including Atuntaqui, and he rebuilt Quito, making it the second capital of the Inca Empire. He built astonishing astronomical observatories, too, along with many strongholds.

It was during Huayna Capac's reign that the Inca empire reached the height of its size and power. During its peak, it stretched over a vast area, including many parts of modern Bolivia, Peru, Argentina, Chile, Ecuador, and the south-west parts of Colombia.

Huayna Capac is believed to have died of measles or smallpox, the deadly weapon the Spanish conquistadors had unwittingly carried with them into the lands of the Inca.

Huáscar (c. 1527-1532 AD)

Although Huáscar was Huayna Capac's legitimate heir, his favourite was Atahualpa. Each son was granted a separate realm of the Inca Empire. Huáscar received the southern part with the capital of Cuzco while Atahualpa was given the northern part with Quito as the capital. Things carried on peacefully for four or five years, and together the two sons may have even been able to take on the Spanish. But this was not meant to be, because Huáscar decided he wanted the entire kingdom for himself, throwing the empire into the terrors of civil war.

Translated from Quechua, his name means 'golden chain.' It is difficult to say whether Huáscar was named as the successor, or if it were the nobles in Cuzco who pushed his claim forward, but the fact remains he wanted to rule over the entire Inca empire.

The Spanish chronicler Juan de Betanzos portrays Huáscar as a tyrannical ruler who seized the wives of his lords if they only took his fancy and similarly seized many Lands of the Sun, showing disrespect for the Inca religion. However, the account may be biased since Betanzo's wife was most likely on Atahualpa's side.

The civil war that followed saw some 60,000 men fight on each side, eventually gaining a victory for Atahualpa. However, it was short-lived.

Atahualpa (1532 - 1533 AD)

When the Spanish conquistadors met the still victorious Atahualpa, he was described as fairly short, robust man with an ear that had been damaged in a battle.

The Incas had lots of depictions of Atahualpa on wooden panels and some portraits and tapestries. These were sent to Spain and unfortunately have since been lost.

It's much easier to account Atahualpa's life events though. After defeating and imprisoning Huáscar, the new Inca Emperor massacred all the pretenders to the throne and burned many of the nobles in Cuzco, including several mummies who had allegedly sworn allegiance to Huáscar. Some accounts even say he ripped out the hearts of his opposers and forced their supporters to eat them.

Naturally, after such an astounding victory, Atahualpa underestimated the threat the Spanish posed, led by Francisco Pizarro. However, the measly Spanish force of some 168 men and 69 horses eventually defeated Atahualpa's grand army. Atahualpa was captured and used by Pizarro to control the empire. He was eventually executed, spurring many claims to the throne. However, the Inca Empire had already started to disintegrate and would remain in the hands of the Spanish for centuries.

Chapter 12 – The Spanish Conquest

Perhaps the most baffling fact about the history of the Incas is how such a vast empire - the biggest that the Americas had ever seen - could have fallen so easily to the Spanish of just 168 men?

It is true that Atahualpa's armies had been significantly weakened by the civil war. However, Atahualpa and his forces were still much more powerful than the Spanish conquistadors. So what happened?

Before the conquistadors finally met with the Incas, the Spanish conquest had been in motion for some time. It started in 1492 and by 1519 the Aztec empire in modern-day Mexico had been defeated. Many of the Spaniards embarked on their mission with the objective to find a great fortune. However, not everyone did, and so they carried on with their quest for gold until they finally came face-to-face with the Incas. In fact, out of Francisco Pizarro's 168 men, only 30 came fresh from Spain. The rest of them had spent 10 or 20 years in Mexico, aiding the conquest. They wanted to make their mark on the world, gain new riches and lands, and they had years of battle experience which made them a small yet dangerous force for the Incas.

Pizarro's first encounter with the New World was in 1513, when he arrived in Panama, accompanying Vasco Núñez de Balboa. His first encounter with the Inca Empire was in 1524, and he made a second attempt in 1526. A combination of inclement weather, hostility from the natives and a lack of support and provisions led to failure. However, in 1531 Pizarro returned and, to his advantage, some of the Inca royal court, including the ruler Huayna Capac, were impacted by the Spanish diseases. What's more, the chaos caused by these deaths allowed Huáscar to start a war against his half-brother Atahualpa.

So the odds were in Pizarro's favour. By 1531 his force had made its way to Ecuador, where they gained a victory in the province of Coaque. There they waited a few months for reinforcements to arrive. During that time, they battled with the many diseases that were rampant on the Ecuadorian coast. Just like the natives were unequipped to deal with European diseases like smallpox and measles, so were the Spanish unequipped to deal with the native diseases. Among these was a disease described by their chroniclers as 'berrugas.'

Nonetheless, the reinforcements arrived, and Pizarro reassembled his army in 1532. They headed southwards. Along the way, the Inca ruler sent presents and an invitation to the Spaniards to visit the ruler's camp. It may appear like a generous gesture, but for the Incas such an invitation held a specific strategic message. This was how the Incas traditionally issued a threat to an enemy. But since the Spaniards missed this cultural queue, they advanced at a steady pace. Nonetheless, the Inca probably didn't think anything much of the Spaniards. In November 1532, Pizarro's army reached Cajamarca, near where Atahualpa was taking some long, relaxing thermal baths, having just defeated Huáscar.

Pizarro's men took refuge from the rain and hailstorm in the buildings surrounding the main plaza in Cajamarca. He sent his men Hernando Pizarro and de Soto to meet Atahualpa in the nearby thermal baths, and to invite him back to Cajamarca to meet with Pizarro. Atahualpa was not very interested at first, but once he discovered Hernando was related to Francisco Pizarro, he even offered to host a dinner for the troop.

However, they declined out of caution. They could not pass on the offer to have a drink together, and during this friendly ceremony the Spaniards put on a grand display of horsemanship. The horse came too close for comfort to Atahualpa, and his servants immediately rebuffed the horse and the Spaniards. Unfortunately, the gesture was not well-received - because Atahualpa had remained passive, he expected the same of his servants. Their loyalty couldn't save them, and all four of the servants were executed.

Atahualpa agreed to meet with the Spanish forces the next day in Cajamarca's main plaza. Pizarro wasn't sure how to proceed - should he pretend his troops were a friendly envoy from Spain? Should he ask the Inca to swear his allegiance to the King of Spain? Or should he cut the talk short and launch a surprise attack? Together with his men, Pizarro decided to delay the decision and make up his mind as the talks progressed.

Nonetheless, his army was able to utilize the surroundings of Cajamarca and hid in the many buildings and corridors that wound around the main plaza. They were big enough to hide not only the soldiers but even the horsemen. The Spanish also had an advantage because they were able to block the narrow entrance and exit points to the square.

The Battle of Cajamarca

After much anxious waiting, Atahualpa finally entered the open space. It was a truly spectacular sight. At first, Atahualpa's guard and servants assembled themselves, dressed in various flashy colours. They swept the road and removed straws from it, clearing the way for their emperor. Then squadrons in different dresses appeared all dancing and singing. Then soldiers wearing metal plates arrived, and finally the emperor himself - Atahualpa in all his splendour, adorned with plate shoulders of gold, whose litter was carried in by several servants.

The Dominican friar, a representative of the Vatican, conveyed the 'true faith' to Atahualpa. Through an interpreter, he presented the Emperor with a Bible that was supposed to convey the word of God and explained to Atahualpa that from now on he'd need to pay tribute to the Emperor Charles V.

Atahualpa was interested in his gift. He examined the book, he put it to his ear and finally, with great difficulty, opened the cover - only to assume that he'd been tricked because he could not understand the writing. Angered, he threw the book on the floor. This was the perfect opportunity for Pizarro to launch his attack, as the friar shouted the Inca had blasphemed against the word of God.

The Spanish acted fast - cannons were fired, exploding in the midst of the packed rows of the Inca soldiers. Horsemen and soldiers on foot soon followed suit. They slaughtered everyone without mercy in the close vicinity of Atahualpa. Within the space of just two hours, 7,000 Inca soldiers lay dead, and their emperor - captured. This marked the start of the demise of the Inca Empire.

As well as possessing some strategic advantages, battle wits and experience that allowed the Spaniards to quickly capture the Inca ruler, what other advantages did they have? In other words, how did the two armies compare in terms of weapons and military gear?

The Spanish army

The Spanish army was experienced in battle, and well-equipped. In addition to their foot soldiers (infantry), they also had something that the Incas did not - horsemen (cavalry). The horsemen received higher rewards for successful campaigns, so most soldiers who fought on foot aspired to buy a horse and become part of the cavalry.

The horsemen fought primarily with lances (long wooden spears with steel or iron points) and swords. The lances were incredibly effective at slaughtering native foot soldiers when used by a rider on a horse. The swords were roughly three feet long, narrow and double-edged (sharp on both sides). The Spanish city of Toledo had a reputation for being one of the best places in the world for making swords and armour. The steel swords produced in Toledo had a huge advantage over the arms used by the natives - so much so that the Spaniards actually prohibited the natives from having these swords years after the conquest.

The Spanish foot soldiers also used long-range weapons, such as the 'harquebus' or a type of early musket, and a crossbow. Although the harquebus was slow to load and heavy to carry, it was effective in instilling fear into the native soldiers because they suspiciously believed that the Spanish had the power to create thunder. The crossbow was equally cumbersome to carry and use in a battle against quick-footed native soldiers, so these were not much used after the initial phases of the conquest. Nonetheless, the favourite weapon of the foot soldiers was undeniably a fine Toledo sword that allowed the Spaniards to defeat dozens of natives within the space of a few frantic minutes.

The Spaniards had another advantage - their armour. Made of impenetrable steel that the natives had not seen before, their armour made the Spanish almost invulnerable in direct combat. Helmets, heavy breastplates, arm and leg greaves, a metal skirt and a gorget to protect the neck, covered the Spanish soldiers from tip to toe. Thus, the natives only rarely killed a Spanish soldier, clad all over in armour, as they did not have any weapons designed to pierce through steel.

Last but not least, the Spanish army had another weapon that the natives did not have - their motivation to fight for their own survival among a foreign enemy, the chance to carve out a name for themselves in history books, the passion to fight for the glory of God, the Christian cause and their king, and the irresistible opportunity to gain wealth and power in the process.

The Inca army

The Inca army was very different to the Spaniards - both in their motives and their weaponry. For many of them, fighting in a battle for an Inca ruler was not even a choice. The Inca army consisted primarily of conscripts who had to use their own weapons, led by their own lords who owed their service as a duty to their state. An army would usually be mobilized during the agricultural off-season, so the many different tribes that formed the Inca army were first and foremost farmers.

These were usually sound and married males, aged 25 to 50, who were called into the army on a rotating basis. They brought their wives and kin along with them to battle, all moving on foot to reach the battlefield. Single men between 18 and 25 usually bore cargo and messages for those who would later fight in the war. The soldiers were organized by their ethnic group, each wearing colourful, distinctive clothes and carrying distinctive weapons. This made it easier to distinguish a friend from a foe during a battle.

However, the Incas did have their own personal guard, drawn from Cuzco's aristocracy and known as 'big ears' for the large earspools that they wore. The Incas also had dedicated societies to soldiery, known as *Chachapoyas*. The guards were usually well-ordered but other than that, the Inca army contained few military specialists.

For the Incas, a battle was a ritual affair. Along with their armour and weapons, they also carried a range of idols with them into the battlefield, known as *wuq'a*. The soldiers who carried arrows, sling stones and javelins for long-range combat usually preceded troops who bore wielded maces, clubs and spears for hand-to-hand combat. The emperor, of course, was carried in a special litter, wielding slings and spears. Nonetheless, the weapons of choice for the Incas were:
- a stone or bronze star mace with a wooden handle;
- a hard, double-edged palmwood club that was shaped like a sword.

As for their armour, the native soldiers wore quilted cloth that was incredibly effective against Andean weapons - so much so that some Spaniards swapped their heavy armour and chose to wear the Inca armour instead to provide lighter protection. The Incas also wore wood or bronze shields and helmets.

Nonetheless, the weapons of the natives were no match to those used by the conquistadors. Some of the natives carried heavy clubs or maces, or stone axes or clubs with spikes on the end. The heavy armour of the Spanish protected well against the blows inflicted by these weapons. The most lethal weapon employed by the natives was a 'macuahuitl'. This was a wooden sword with obsidian shards on either side - nonetheless, it was no match for the Spanish steel armour or Toledo blade, and a Spanish soldier could easily slay a dozen natives while only receiving a few scratches or bruises in return.

The capture of Atahualpa

Mockingly, Pizarro invited the Inca Emperor to have dinner with him in captivity. It soon dawned on Atahualpa what the Spaniards were after - treasure. He offered to fill an entire room, full with treasure - twice over with silver objects and once over with gold. Pizarro liked the idea and agreed to wait things out until the Inca Emperor fulfilled his promise. In fact, this was beneficial to both parties - the Spanish were able to wait for reinforcements and Atahualpa carried on organising court and making plans for his escape. It was a tricky situation for the Spanish as their tiny force in Cajamarca was surrounded by tens of thousands of Inca armies, who were unsure as to how best to free their leader.

Nonetheless, they were able to explore the lands beyond Cajamarca under a royal order. In fact, the Incas even carried three of the Spanish soldiers on litters all the way to the Inca capital of Cuzco. During this trip, they met with Huáscar, the defeated Inca prince. Naturally, he offered the Spanish to join forces with him and promised to make them rich beyond belief, if they agreed to help his cause. But the Spanish refused, and soon after Atahualpa heard word of this and ordered for Huáscar to be executed.

By April, the Spanish reinforcements had arrived. Equally, Atahualpa had fulfilled his promise and filled an entire room (about 7m wide and 5m tall) with gold and two more rooms with silver.

Since they now had a fortune of about $50 million, the Spanish decided the Inca ruler was no longer of any use to them. Pizarro, however, had grown fond of Atahualpa - he'd learned how to play chess, and they dined together frequently. He wasn't sure what to do, as Atahualpa could be useful as a prisoner. Nonetheless, the growing tensions among the Spanish demanded his execution.

A court was conducted, and Atahualpa was convicted of 12 charges, including treason. He was accused of killing his brother and also plotting against Pizarro. He was offered to be burned at the stake or executed by garrote if he became a Christian. Because he needed his body for his own religious beliefs, Atahualpa opted to become a Christian. On July 26, 1533, the last independent Inca ruler was executed by garrote.

After Atahualpa's death

Although Pizarro was somewhat forced into deciding to execute Atahualpa due to the growing discontent among the Spanish forces, not everyone agreed with it. King Charles seemed to have been displeased with Atahualpa's execution since he was a monarch and had to be treated as such. He was called back to Spain to explain himself.

The Incas were confused and divided. Atahualpa's supporters were naturally upset and despaired. But Huáscar's supporters were delighted. The Spanish now needed a 'puppet' to rule on their behalf, and they installed the younger brother of Huáscar and Atahualpa, called Túpac Huallpa. Along the way from Cajamarca to Cuzco, this new ruler died of a disease.

With or without a leader, the Spaniards carried on their journey to Cuzco. There, another Inca prince Manco Inca Yupanqui joined their quest. Together, they marched on Cuzco, a year to the day since their first encounter in Cajamarca.

Three years later, Manco Inca Yupanqui was tired of co-ruling with the Spanish. They had thrown a lot of the nobles out of their homes, they were disrespectful towards the Inca culture, and he wanted to rule independently. So he escaped Cuzco, with plans to raise an army and defeat the Spaniards. He succeeded and raised an army between 200,000 and 400,000 men and attacked the Spanish forces in Cuzco. But despite his best efforts - Manco Inca Yupanqui tried to burn the city, then flood it - the Spanish resisted. Soon, the great Inca army began to disintegrate - it had been formed of local farmers who had to return home to attend to their crop. After ten long months of siege, Manco Inca Yupanqui retreated, founding a Neo-Inca state in the remote jungles of Vilcabamba. It would last until the death of the last independent Inca ruler Túpac Amaru in 1572.

Conclusion

The Spanish did not possess any superpowers, nor did they have a massive force behind them. Their success was down to some circumstances that fell in their favour, paired with their military experience and motivation to fight for God and glory.

1. The civil war between Atahualpa and Huáscar weakened the Inca armies and split the Inca empire into two parts - it was not united when the Spanish arrived. Thus, almost half of the Inca population (those on Huáscar's side) saw the Spanish as their saviours and were ready to join them to fight Atahualpa. In addition, since the Inca Empire ruled over many native tribes and cultures, many of the locals hated the Incas and wanted to see them be overthrown and liberated from their oppressors.

2. Atahualpa's recent success made him underestimate the threat that the Spanish posed. Preoccupied with fighting Huáscar, he missed many opportunities to attack the relatively small Spanish force.

3. The Spanish had advantages in the arms they carried and the armour they wore. They also had horsemen - this was absolutely new to the Incas whose armies always moved on foot.

4. The Incas had been weakened by European diseases, such as smallpox and measles.

5. The Andean army was not always happy to be fighting. It was formed of farmers who were unskilled soldiers, compared to the Spaniards. They completed their service as a tax and had to go back to their crops when the agricultural season was up. Therefore they were not fit for a long-term war. The Spanish army, on the other hand, consisted of seasoned warriors, most of whom had spent decades fighting in Mexico and only a fraction of their men were fresh from Spain. And their motive was possibly their biggest asset - the Spanish were fighting for their own wealth, power and glory, the glory of their King and their God.

6. After Atahualpa's death, the Incas did not have a strong leader. Since the Incas had ruled over many native tribes, the population remained fractured.

Chapter 13 - The Aftermath and the Inca Legacy

Once the Inca Empire and the Neo-Inca state had been successfully defeated, a civil war broke out among the Spanish. In 1541, Francisco Pizarro himself was assassinated by his opponent Diego de Almagro II's men. He was later killed, too. The last Spanish civil war ended in 1554. Thus, for the first 20 years of the conquest, there was no order in the Inca Empire. These are remembered as the 'Black years' by the locals, with many of the local ethnic groups having lost 50% of their population.

All this changed when Viceroy Francisco de Toledo came to power in 1570-72. He moved large numbers of the Andean people out of their traditional communities and into new settlements the Spanish could more easily control. Thus, eliminating the independence, the locals had achieved.

The changing history

Soon it dawned on the locals they were far worse off under the Spanish rule than they had been under the rule of the Incas, so they staged a great number of rebellions (20 to 30 within 150 years). The Spanish prevailed. This is likely when the legends of the Incas were born that presented them in a glorious light.

The local Andeans began to talk about the 'good old times,' omitting details of the oppressive nature of the Inca rule. A whole series of myths emerged, surrounding the return of Inkarrí, an Inca Emperor who would free them of their bonds. This myth is still present today.

The Spanish and their interpretation

The Spanish conquistadors had their part to play in the shaping of the Inca history. When it came to the Inca religion, for example, their priests could only use their Christian faith to reference the Inca and the Andean religions. Therefore, they called the Inca temples 'mosques' because they had not seen anything else. Equally, their priests went to great pains to interpret the local Andean religion in a way that it aligned with the Christian theology. For instance, the flood that the Andean locals mentioned in their myths was interpreted as the Biblical flood.

Only 10 to 15 years after the conquest did the Spanish priests begin to inquire more thoroughly about the local Andean and Inca religions. However, this served the purpose of stamping out their different world views and religious rites, rather than genuinely trying to understand the significance of these rites in the Inca society. By the time their interest became genuine, the Incas had learned to celebrate their rites in secrecy and no longer shared this knowledge with the Spaniards.

The Inca Legacy Today

Remarkably, even all these years after the Spanish conquest, the native Andean people continue to observe many ancient rites and rituals. For example, the people of Cuzco reinstate the June Summer Solstice festival each year with a great ceremony.

The cycles and myths of Inkarrí continue to this day, as the local Andean population, especially among the communities in the Peruvian highlands, who still follow the traditional lifestyle and yearn for the 'good old days.' These people observe the cycles of nature, as their forefathers did before them, and they have a reverence for the sky and the earth, as expressed in their annual practices and ceremonies.

During the 1980s, the Peruvian national currency was called Inti (after the Inca sun god), and today's currency is called Sol, the Spanish name for 'sun.'

The Peruvian election in 2000 is an excellent example of the Inca ideologies that remain potent among the local communities even today. The Inca population raged a series of protests surrounding the presidential election in Peru in 2000. A huge rally was staged in Lima surrounding the political process, and the name given to the rally was 'The March of the Four Parts.' One could just as easily call it 'The March of the Inca Empire.'

Conclusion

Even after so many hundreds of years have passed since the last Inca ruler died, the ancient Inca traditions remain alive today. The local farmers in the Peruvian highlands are still very much connected to the earth and the movements of the sky, which they used to predict the outcome of their crops. That knowledge is perhaps one of the most beautiful aspects of Inca legacy today.

Just as the traditions remain true, so does the yearning to be free people. Any debate about the negative aspects of modern day politics in the modern Peru stirs within the locals strong feelings of once being part of the greatest empire the Americas ever saw.

However, much of this nostalgia may be tainted from the truth of the events. As much as the Inca Empire has been portrayed as a wonderful utopia in many historical accounts, where life was good, this version of the truth likely emerged after the locals felt the price of the Spanish conquest. The Inca Empire was far more than just a stereotype of a perfect kingdom. The story of the Inca Empire is one of 'greys' - ever-shifting perceptions and loyalties, on the backdrop of rigid social norms and customs. It is a history filled with dynastic wars among relatively short periods of peace that eventually served to lead to its demise. To know what a local Inca felt during any one of these periods, or what he thought of his empire, remains a mystery that, even with so much evidence presented, we can guess at best.

If you enjoyed this book, then I'd really appreciate it if you would post a short review on Amazon. I read all the reviews myself so that I can continue to provide books that people want. Thanks for your support!

Check out another book by Captivating History

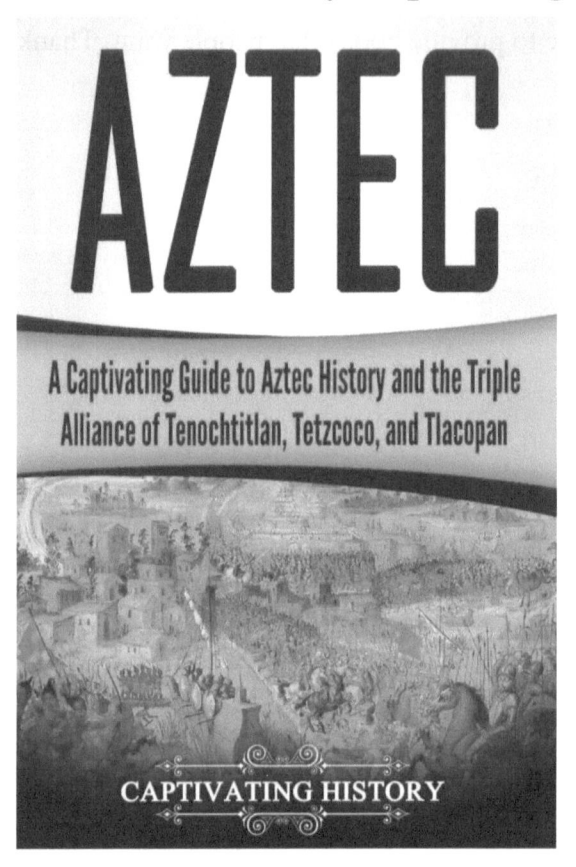

Free Bonus from Captivating History (Available for a Limited time)

Hi History Lovers!

Now you have a chance to join our exclusive history list so you can get your first history ebook for free as well as discounts and a potential to get more history books for free! Simply visit the link below to join.

Captivatinghistory.com/ebook

Also, make sure to follow us on:

Twitter: @Captivhistory

Facebook: Captivating History: @captivatinghistory

Endnotes

Introduction:

- Cartwright, Mark. *Inca Civilization*. [Online]. Available from: https://www.ancient.eu/Inca_Civilization/. Accessed 20 September 2017.

- D'Altroy, Professor Terence N. *The Incas: Inside and American Empire*. Audio book and course guide. 2004. Recorded Books, LLC. (Various lectures from this resource have been used throughout the following chapters.)

Chapter 1:

- First People Website. *Viracocha and the Coming of the Incas*. [Online]. Available from: https://www.bibliotecapleyades.net/arqueologia/viracocha01.htm Accessed 3 October 2017.

- Cartwright, Mark. *Viracocha*. [Online]. Available from: https://www.ancient.eu/Viracocha/. Accessed 25 September 2017.

- Minster, Cristopher. *Viracocha and the Legendary Origins of the Inca*. 2006. [Online]. Available from: https://www.thoughtco.com/viracocha-and-legendary-origins-of-inca-2136321 Accessed October 15, 2017

Chapter 3:

- Benjamin S. Orlove et al. *Forecasting Andean rainfall and crop yield from the influence of El Niño on Pleiades visibility*. 2000. [Online]. Available from: http://www.nature.com/nature/journal/v403/n6765/full/403068a0.html?foxtrotcallback=true Accessed October 15, 2017

- Minster, Cristipher. *The Dark Constellations of the Inca Empire*. 2017. [Online]. Available from: https://www.thoughtco.com/inca-star-worship-and-constellations-2136315 Accessed October 12, 2017.

- Urton, Gary. *Animals and Astronomy in the Quechua*

Universe. Proceedings from the American Philosophical Society (Vol. 125, No. 2). 1981. [Online] Available from: http://fcaglp.fcaglp.unlp.edu.ar/~sixto/arqueo/curso/Urton%20-%20Animals%20and%20Astronomy%20in%20the%20Quechua%20Universe.pdf Accessed October 5, 2017.

Chapter 4:

- Encyclopaedia Britannica. *Andean Civilizations.* [Online]. Available from: https://www.britannica.com/topic/pre-Columbian-civilizations/Andean-civilization#ref583694 Accessed October 15, 2017.

- Encyclopaedia Britannica. *Inca People.* [Online]. Available from: https://www.britannica.com/topic/Inca#ref5926 Accessed October 15, 2017.

- Foerster, Brien. *Inca Rule: A Brief Timeline From Rise To Ruin Of A Great Civilization.* [Online]. Available from: https://hiddenincatours.com/inca-rule-a-brief-timeline-from-rise-to-ruin-of-a-great-civilization/ Accessed October 5, 2017.

Chapter 6:

- *The Secrets Of The Incas - Part 1 of 2.* Timeline: World History Documentaries. [Online]. Available from: https://www.youtube.com/watch?v=oRSTy9ir6zs Accessed October 5, 2017

- *The Secrets Of The Incas - Part 2 of 2.* Timeline: World History Documentaries. [Online]. Available from: https://www.youtube.com/watch?v=Kkdj39R3bAs Accessed October 5, 2017.

- Dr. Sullivan, William L. *The Secret of the Incas: Myth, Astronomy and the War Against Time.* 1997, Broadway Books.

Chapter 8:

- *Incan Women.* [Online]. Available from: http://www2.ivcc.edu/gender2001/Incan_Women.htm Accessed October 10, 2017.

- Echegaray, Luis Olivera. *The Inca Chosen Women and the Acllahuasi*. [Online]. Available from: http://cuzcoeats.com/inca-chosen-women-acllahuasi/
- *Gender roles in Inca Society*. [Online]. Available from: http://kendallkpsd401.weebly.com/uploads/4/0/3/7/40379583/gender_roles_in_inca_society.pdf Accessed October 5, 2017.

Chapter 9:

- *The Inca Pantheoon*. [Online] Available from: http://www.mythicjourneys.org/bigmyth/myths/english/eng_inca_pantheon.htm Accessed October 6, 2017
- *Inca Human Sacrifice*. [Online]. Available from: http://mayaincaaztec.com/inhusa.html Accessed October 7, 2017.
- *Inti Raymi, The Celebration of the Sun*. [Online]. Available from: http://www.discover-peru.org/inti-raymi/ Accessed October 10, 2017

Chapter 10:

- *10 Most Impressive Ancient Inca Ruins*. [Online]. Available from: http://www.touropia.com/ancient-inca-ruins/ Accessed October 17, 2017
- Reed, Drew. *Coricancha, the Incas' temple of the sun: a history of cities in 50 buildings, day 3*. The Guardian. [Online]. Available from: https://www.theguardian.com/cities/2015/mar/25/cusco-coricancha-temple-history-cities-50-buildings Accessed October 16, 2017.

Chapter 12:

- Minster, Christopher. *Armor and Weapons of the Spanish Conquistadors*. Thought.co. [Online]. Available from: https://www.thoughtco.com/armor-and-weapons-of-spanish-conquistadors-2136508 Accessed November 3, 2017
- D'Altroy, Professor Terence N. *Lecture 5: Inca Militarism*. The Incas: Inside and American Empire. Audio book and course guide. 2004. Recorded Books, LLC.

ABOUT CAPTIVATING HISTORY

A lot of history books just contain dry facts that will eventually bore the reader. That's why Captivating History was created. Now you can enjoy history books that will mesmerize you. But be careful though, hours can fly by, and before you know it; you're up reading way past bedtime.

Get your first history book for free here:
http://www.captivatinghistory.com/ebook

Make sure to follow us on Twitter: @CaptivHistory
and Facebook: www.facebook.com/captivatinghistory so you can get all of our updates!

Made in United States
Troutdale, OR
10/07/2024

23504651R00050